Getting to Know the REAL YOU

50 Fun Quizzes
Just for Girls

Harriet S. Mosatche, Ph.D., and
Elizabeth K. Lawner

PRIMA PUBLISHING

Published by Prima Publishing, Roseville, California. Member of the Crown Publishing Group, a division of Random House, Inc.

PRIMA PUBLISHING and colophon are trademarks of Random House, Inc., registered with the United States Patent and Trademark Office.

Library of Congress Cataloging-in-Publication Data

Mosatche, Harriet S.

Getting to know the real you : 50 fun quizzes just for girls / Harriet S. Mosatche and Elizabeth K. Lawner

v. cm.

Includes index.

ISBN 0-7615-2954-3

1. Girls—Psychology—Miscellanea. 2. Teenage girls—Psychology—Miscellanea. 3. Interpersonal relations in adolescence—Miscellanea. 4. Questions and answers. I. Lawner, Elizabeth K. II. Title.

HQ777.M578 2002

305.23—dc21 2002066283

02 03 04 05 06 HH 10 9 8 7 6 5 4 3 2

Printed in the United States of America

First Edition

Visit us online at www.primapublishing.com

Contents

Introduction

Wouldn't you like to get to know yourself better? Have you thought about how you deal with people problems or manage your time, or how far you'd go to be popular? What about how you relate to friends, guys, teachers, and parents? By taking the quizzes in this book, you'll learn lots more about yourself and have fun doing it, too. Both of us have always liked taking quizzes in magazines, and we had a great time writing them for you. And if you find out some things about yourself that are maybe less than flattering, we'll give you tips that can help you change your style and your world.

While you're discovering more about yourself, we thought we should share a little about ourselves, too. At the end of each quiz, along with an explanation of the scoring and a listing of the tips, you'll see a "Harriet Says" or "Liz Says" section, or both. That's where we admit, confirm, confess, and remember interesting, embarrassing, personal, and true tidbits about ourselves. We hope these will let you see us as the only-too-human people we are, with our fair share of humiliating moments, bad judgments, and shining accomplishments. They add up to pieces of us, not the whole picture, but enough to give you a good idea about where we stand and what we're like.

Before you grab that pen or pencil to take your first quiz, we want to formally introduce ourselves.

Harriet says: I have to admit I haven't been a teen in a long time, but believe me, I have vivid memories of those years. I'm just one of those adults who has never forgotten what it's like to be your age, which helps when you're a developmental psychologist, which is what I am. Besides, my daughter is thirteen and my son is sixteen, and they and their friends keep me very connected to the teen world. And, I've been giving advice to preteens and teens since 1997 on the Girl Scout Web site ("Ask Dr. M" at www.girlscouts.org). Girls from all over the world write to me for advice, asking everything from what to do about their annoying siblings to the best way to get boys to notice them. My daughter and coauthor, Liz, answers many of the questions, too.

This is the second book Liz and I have worked on together. The first was *Girls: What's So Bad About Being Good? How to Have Fun, Survive the Preteen Years, and Remain True to Yourself*, and from that experience, we learned that we're not a bad team.

Liz says: My most important qualification for writing this book is that I'm a young teen. I like giving advice, both online and in person, to my friends. I love taking quizzes, and I've learned that I also like to create new ones. You can be sure that every quiz in this book is Liz-tested, partly because I wanted to know how I scored and partly to make sure it would work with girls your age.

When I'm not writing quizzes, I'm usually dancing. In fact, some of the time while I was thinking about how to construct particular questions, I was dancing around my computer. Of course, I also go to school—I'm in the eighth grade. And I love hanging out or talking on the telephone with my friends. Just like you, I get more homework than I'd like, argue with my parents sometimes and with my brother more of the time, and am passionate about music—yes, I do listen while I'm doing my homework.

We divided this book into ten chapters, each one focusing on a different theme, from your feelings to your friendships and from your body to the boys in your life. You don't have to go through the chapters or the quizzes in any particular order. We want you to have fun while you're learning about yourself. Be honest as you take these quizzes—that's the only way you'll really learn the truth about yourself. And make sure you read and follow some of the tips—in other words, challenge yourself to become the best you can be!

CHAPTER 1

What Makes You *You*?

Is your self-esteem way up in the stratosphere, down in the subbasement level, or somewhere in between? Are you courageous enough to take a serious risk now and then, or do you hide from anything that might even hint at the unknown? You'll be clued in to the answers to these questions as well as other equally important ones by taking the quizzes in this chapter. So if you want to know more about what really makes you *you*, get your pen or pencil out, and start making some choices.

Is Your Self-Esteem Sky-High or Down in the Dumps?

High self-esteem means that you feel good about yourself and your abilities. Are you confident enough to find out where your self-esteem stands?

1. *When your English teacher calls on you in class, you:*
   ___ a. begin by saying, "I'm not really sure, but the answer might be . . . "
   ___ b. speak in a clear, confident voice.
   ✓ c. state the answer quickly and quietly even though you know your answer's right.

2. *The boy who sits behind you in science class calls you at home. You think:*
   ___ a. he probably likes me.
   ✓ b. he probably tried a dozen other kids first, and no one was home.
   ___ c. he was probably calling on a dare.

3. *You've just turned in a term paper you worked very hard on. You:*
   ___ a. are afraid your teacher will fail you.
   ___ b. assume you'll be receiving at least a B+, and maybe an A.
   ✓ c. expect to get a passing grade.

4. *When a new girl about your age moves into your neighborhood, you:*
   ___ a. think she'll probably have more friends than you have in a matter of weeks.
   ✓ b. want to meet her to see if the two of you might become friends.
   ___ c. are sure she'll like you once she gets to know you.

5. *Your gym teacher has demonstrated a new game. You:*
   ✓ a. are not sure that you want to play, but since the aerobics stuff you've been doing has gotten boring, you're willing to give it a try.
   ___ b. can't wait to play the new game—you're always up for trying something new.

___ c. hide behind some other kids hoping you won't have to play until you're sure you understand all the rules and won't make a fool of yourself.

6. *Your best friend has invited you to a party. You decide to wear:*
   ___ a. the loudest outfit you own so the other guests can't possibly miss you when you arrive.
   ✓ b. your usual jeans and T-shirt.
   ___ c. your new top with spaghetti straps.

7. *When you get your report card, you:*
   ___ a. are shocked by how much higher your grades are than what you had expected.
   ✓ b. aren't surprised at all by your grades—you pretty much figured out how well you'd do.
   ___ c. don't even want to look at how you've done.

8. *When your guidance counselor at school asks you to complete a personality test honestly, you write:*
   ✓ a. "I really like myself, even though there are a couple of things I might work on."
   ___ b. "I think I'm okay, but I really need to change about three or four basic characteristics."
   ___ c. "Help! I need a complete personality overhaul."

9. *When some of your friends are discussing a new music video at lunch, most of them comment that they really liked it. You hated it. You say:*
   ___ a. nothing. Why bother giving your opinion?
   ___ b. "Yeah, I liked it, too," but without a lot of enthusiasm. Why give them something to argue with you about?
   ✓ c. "Actually, I didn't like it at all" and then proceed to explain that the violence in the video concerns you.

10. *You've just gotten a part-time job after school. You can really use the money, but one thing bothers you—your boss never pays you quite what you're owed. You:*
   ✓ a. calmly let your boss know that if she expects you to work the extra time, you need to get paid for it.
   ___ b. decide to focus on the positive aspects of the job and stop thinking about the few dollars owed you.
   ___ c. get so resentful about what your boss is doing that you stop putting your best effort into the work and start spending your time gossiping with coworkers instead.

Scoring

1. a: 1; b: 3; c: 2
2. a: 3; b: 1; c: 1
3. a: 1; b: 3; c: 2
4. a: 1; b: 2; c: 3
5. a: 2; b: 3; c: 1
6. a: 3; b: 1; c: 2
7. a: 1; b: 3; c: 1
8. a: 3; b: 2; c: 1
9. a: 2; b: 1; c: 3
10. a: 3; b: 2; c: 1

10–15 points: Self-Esteem Needs Work. Here are some tips for you to try so you'll like yourself better:

- Tell yourself that you like yourself—at least five times a day. Even if you don't mean it at first, this kind of positive self-talk (that's what talking to yourself is officially called) will affect how you see yourself—eventually.

Liz Says:

A few years ago when I was about ten years old, my self-esteem was lower than it is now. I almost never raised my hand in class and always talked really quietly. Everyone knew that I was quiet, and when I had to read a paragraph in class about being aggressive, I could tell that all the kids were trying not to laugh. At age thirteen, I still have to work at building my self-esteem, but the progress I've made so far has encouraged me to keep at it.

- Do at least one nice thing for yourself every day—you're worth it. Maybe these actions will convince you that you're a pretty important person.
- Make a list of ten of your most special qualities. Put the list where you'll notice it often.
- Enlist a friend or family member in your quest to raise your self-esteem. Ask that person to remind you when you're not taking credit when you should or belittling your looks or acting ill at ease.

16–20 points: Decent Self-Esteem. You're doing okay in the self-esteem department, but trying the tips above might boost it even higher.

21–30 points: Sky-High Self-Esteem. You like yourself—a lot. That's great, as long as you're being honest. But being "the star" all the time can get exhausting. Try taking a back seat once in a while to allow friends to shine, too.

Do You Let Your Imagination Soar?

Your imagination helps you solve problems and have fun. Is yours taking off or keeping you behind?

1. *Your health education teacher asks you to do an antismoking project. You can choose what you're going to do. You:*
   - ___ a. immediately have an anxiety attack since the project is too unstructured for you.
   - X b. think of two or three ways to complete the project and choose to interview people who were able to successfully stop smoking.
   - ___ c. close your eyes and imagine several attention-getting ways to make your point, and then decide on a series of cartoons filled with characters who have made different choices about smoking.

2. *When you decide how to put outfits together, you:*
   - ___ a. keep coming up with new combinations since it's boring to always pair your khakis with the same old shirt.
   - X b. are usually a creature of habit—only once in a while do you experiment with new looks.
   - ___ c. are embarrassed to admit it, but you still let your mom prepare your clothes since she knows more about colors and styles than you do.

3. *You're finally going to be thirteen. It's time for a birthday celebration. What do your party plans look like?*
   - X a. since you usually celebrate with a quiet party at home, you decide to do something different to start off your teen years—a bowling party with a few of

your best friends, topped off with an ice cream cake decorated in your favorite colors.

___ b. your three closest friends get to your house before dawn so you can see the sun rise. Then you all put your wishes for your teen years into a time capsule and bury them. It's on to pizza for breakfast before going back to sleep to rest up for more partying in the evening hours.

___ c. why change the way you celebrate? You have your usual party with lots of people and tons of food.

4. *If a friend of yours were asked to describe you, what would she or he most likely say?*

X a. "She's the totally dependable type—definitely not someone to ever surprise me with a crazy idea."

___ b. "I'm never prepared enough for the wild schemes she keeps coming up with."

___ c. "Every once in a while, she does something really different, but most of the time she's pretty predictable."

5. *You receive two party invitations from friends for the same night. You:*

X a. accept the one from the friend you're closest to.

___ b. figure out how you can get to both in the same evening—you've always been good at coming up with crazy plans, and sometimes they actually work.

___ c. try to convince one of the party givers to postpone her party so you won't miss any of the fun.

6. *You have one minute to list here as many words as you can think of from the letters in the word* IMAGINATION.

Ice	Apple	Onion
magic	Grampa	Ticks

 Imagination

Ice cream
needles
Geese
Aborn

7. *You have one minute to list unusual uses for a safety pin.*

Nai picker,

8. *Take another minute to list unusual uses for a nail file.*

Picking out something from a light thing

9. *Make something useful out of three rubber bands, two pencils, and two other objects. You have five minutes to complete it.*

Scoring

You get two bonus points if it didn't bother you at all that this quiz had nine questions (instead of the usual even number of questions) and one bonus point if you only thought about it for a moment.

3

1. a:1; b: 2; c: 3
2. a: 3; b: 2; c: 1
3. a: 2; b: 3; c: 1
4. a: 1; b: 3; c: 2
5. a: 1; b: 3; c: 2
6. 1 point for every three words you listed
7. 1 point for every use listed
8. 1 point for every use listed
9. 1 point if the time passed and you're still staring at all the objects; 2 points if you started working on something; 3 points if you created something that you can actually use.

12 points or fewer: You're Stifling Your Imagination. Here are some tips to help you loosen up and free your creative urges:

- Don't keep relying on doing the same old things in the same old ways. Set a goal to do one imaginative thing each day—whether it's the way you wear your hair or the way you wrap a gift.
- Dream up lots of solutions to a problem before plunging into a situation with the first idea that comes to mind. Brainstorming will give you lots of possibilities instead of just one. That's important whether you're planning a party or deciding on a topic for a school paper.
- Practice brainstorming alone—you could make a list or talk into a tape recorder. And practice with others. Someone else's ideas might spur your thinking in new and interesting directions.
- Create some activities similar to numbers 6, 7, 8, and 9 in this quiz. Do them on your own and with friends. They're fun and they really will help you become more imaginative. Even coming up with the questions is an exercise in building creativity.

Harriet Says:

When I was in seventh grade, boredom with my English class assignments had really gotten to me. So when my teacher asked us to write a report on a magazine article about a foreign country, I decided to do something a bit more creative instead. I made up a country—a small island in the Pacific—and a new magazine, which I called *The Philadelphia Traveler.* (Since I lived in New York City, I thought that Philadelphia was far enough away to make discovery of my deception less probable. Thinking back, *The San Diego Traveler* would have been a safer bet.) To complete my task, I made up the title of the article and the author's name as well. The assignment I had given myself was actually a lot harder than the one the teacher had assigned, since I had to research lots of islands in the Pacific to find out what would sound right. The teacher never figured out what I had done, or at least she never let on. Now, I'm not saying that what I had done was a particularly good use of my creativity, nor is it something I would recommend. Besides, it would be harder today to get away with doing what I did—checking up magazine and country names on the Internet is an easy way these days to uncover the truth.

13–19 points: Your Imagination Is Flying. But it wouldn't hurt to let it soar just a bit higher. You, too, would benefit by following the tips on page 9.

20 and up: You Have a Powerful Imagination. Just don't think you always have to concoct the most outrageous suggestions. Every once in a while, dull and routine can be very comforting.

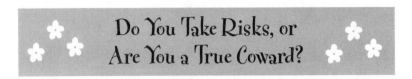

Do You Take Risks, or Are You a True Coward?

Are you courageous enough to take positive risks, or do you typically take the chicken's way out? If you're brave enough to find out, start answering these questions.

1. *At a sleepover party when you're playing Truth or Dare, you're dared to go into your friend's brother's room and act like you're a sleepwalker. You:*
   X a. say, "No way," and tell a truth instead.
   ___ b. go into your friend's brother's room, take a few very quiet steps, and leave quickly.
   ___ c. go into your friend's brother's room, walk around the whole room bumping into things (including your friend's brother), and add some extra loud snoring, too.

2. *On a class trip, you go to the Empire State Building. When you get to the top, you:*
   X a. go out on deck and look out over the edge for a minute and point out some cool buildings.
   ___ b. wait inside next to the elevator until your class comes back.
   ___ c. lean way over the edge until your teacher makes you stop because you're making him nervous.

3. *For an English project, you have to make a presentation on Shirley Temple, which includes having to dress up as her. You show up to school wearing:*
   ___ a. an outrageous polka-dot dress, tap shoes, and a wig.
   ___ b. an old-fashioned party dress and a pair of high heel shoes
   X c. your regular school clothes.

4. *You're invited to a party and none of your friends are invited. In fact you don't know anyone who's invited. You:*
   ___ a. decide not to go. You would never go somewhere where you don't know anyone.
   ___ b. go to the party, dance wildly, and talk to some people you don't know.
   X c. reluctantly go, but barely dance and don't talk to anyone except the hostess.

5. *You go with your best friend to the pool at her beach club. The lifeguard is really hot. You:*
   X a. play Marco Polo anyway. Who cares what he thinks, even though he is hot?
   ___ b. tell your best friend you don't feel like swimming because the water's too cold (even though it's 95 degrees in the shade) and just sit on the side of the pool.
   ___ c. go in the water but don't play the silly games that you were going to play.

6. *You love to play tennis and your parents found a great tennis camp for you to go to, but none of the girls you know are going. You:*
   X a. go anyway but take a while to loosen up.
   ___ b. don't go. What would you do at camp without any friends from home?

___ c. take advantage of this great opportunity, knowing you're going to make some new friends who will share your passion for tennis.

7. *There's a magic show at your school assembly. When the magician asks for volunteers, you:*

X a. don't raise your hand at all. What if they called on you? It would be so embarrassing.

___ b. raise your hand high in the air and wave it around screaming "Pick me, pick me!"

___ c. raise your hand timidly—you're not really sure you want to be called on, but it could be kind of cool.

8. *You love animals and wish there was an animals club at your school. One of your friends tells you that you should try to start the club since you care so much about animals. You:*

___ a. convince one of your other friends to go to the principal's office to ask about starting an animals club.

___ b. go to the principal's office the next day and explain why there should be an animals club.

X c. tell your friend you would never have the guts to talk to the principal. You wait until someone else thinks of the bright idea to start an animals club—then join.

9. *You're on vacation with your family, and they've decided they're all going up a mountain so they can see the beautiful view at the top. The only problem is you have to go on a donkey up a very steep incline, and there are no guides with you. You:*

___ a. tell your family you'll wait at the bottom and look at the photos of the view once they've been developed—you have a book you wanted to finish anyway.

X b. enjoy the great view as you go up the mountain and do a little dance when you get to the top.

___ c. go up but scream so much on the way up that the people next to you ask if you're having a heart attack.

10. *A new girl at your school seems like she would be a fun friend. You:*

X a. ask one of your friends who already knows her to introduce you to her.

___ b. convince yourself she'd never want to be friends with you, and so you just keep hanging out with the group you've known since kindergarten.

Liz Says:

I decided to take this quiz and was a little bit surprised at my score. I thought that I'd end up as a "True Coward," but I was actually "Sometimes a Risk Taker." The one risk that I took that stands out in my mind is question 3, a situation taken right from my life. What really happened was that I had to do a report for English on Shirley Temple and dress up as her. Since I was doing my report on her years as a child, I dressed up in a costume similar to one she wore in a movie she made. I wore a white flowered dress, curled my hair, and even made up a tap dance to go with my presentation. I was a little embarrassed at having my hair in huge curls and wearing an old-fashioned dress to school, but it was worth it when I heard all the compliments on my presentation.

___ c. introduce yourself when you see her in the school cafeteria and start talking to her.

SCORING

1. a: 1; b: 2; c: 3
2. a: 2; b: 1; c: 3
3. a: 3, b: 2, c: 1
4. a: 1; b: 3; c: 2
5. a: 3; b: 1; c: 2
6. a: 2; b: 1; c: 3
7. a: 1; b: 3; c: 2
8. a: 2; b: 3; c: 1
9. a: 1; b: 3; c: 2
10. a: 2; b: 1; c: 3

10–16 points: True Coward. You don't take many risks even if they are risks that can't hurt you physically. You tend to be very careful about your decisions and your actions. That can be a good thing when you're in a potentially dangerous situation, but that overly cautious attitude can also get in the way of fun and adventure. Try these tips:

- Start becoming less of a coward by taking small risks, the kind that might, if something went wrong, just result in a few seconds of embarrassment.
- Try to go with the flow instead of worrying about what might happen. You really don't have to imagine every single possible negative consequence.
- Try one new thing every day. In a few weeks you'll be doing things you never thought you had the guts to do.
- The reason you don't take risks may be that you don't want all eyes on you. Forcing yourself to do things that will make you the center of attention in small groups

will help you get over your social fears. After a while, you can try out your new attitude in larger groups.

17–23 points: Sometimes a Risk Taker. You take risks when they don't have serious consequences. People might laugh, you might be embarrassed, and you won't necessarily meet with success, but your risks don't get you into trouble. They allow you to experiment and have fun.

24–30 points: Bold Babe. You are a wild child and never think twice when taking risks. Unfortunately, too many and the wrong kinds of risks could put you in danger and may jeopardize your health and safety. Think about the following:

- Risk taking can be exciting, but it's no longer fun when you get hurt. Try taking risks that can't hurt you physically.
- You don't always have to be the one everyone has their eyes on. Try to let others have their moment in the spotlight, too.

Are You Open-Minded?

For the statements or situations described here, decide whether you strongly disagree, disagree, agree, or strongly agree with each one. It's going to be hard for you to be totally honest, but do your best. You'll learn more about yourself that way!

1. *You've never seen Jessie wear more than three different outfits to school. You think that if her parents worked harder, the family wouldn't be so poor.*
   - ❑ Strongly disagree
   - ❑ Disagree

- [x] Agree
- [ ] Strongly agree

2. *When your family goes to a new restaurant, you like to try something new.*
   - [ ] Strongly disagree
   - [x] Disagree
   - [ ] Agree
   - [ ] Strongly agree

3. *If one of your best friends told you not to be friends with the new girl at school, you would probably avoid that girl since it's easier that way.*
   - [x] Strongly disagree
   - [ ] Disagree
   - [ ] Agree
   - [ ] Strongly agree

4. *Amelia has been your best friend for ages. She's running against Damika in the school election. You actually think Damika would do a better job, but your loyalty has you voting for Amelia.*
   - [x] Strongly disagree
   - [ ] Disagree
   - [ ] Agree
   - [ ] Strongly agree

5. *When you pop into your aunt's house, she tells you that she has just two pieces left of a delicious chocolate cake—one for you and one for you to bring home to your brother. You figure he won't know that you saved the smaller piece for him. After all, it is your favorite cake, and you could have eaten both slices.*
   - [ ] Strongly disagree
   - [ ] Disagree
   - [x] Agree
   - [ ] Strongly agree

6. *I am willing to boycott (not buy) a product I really like (like my favorite brand of sneakers) if I know it's been produced by children forced to work in terrible conditions in another country.*
   - ❑ Strongly disagree
   - ❑ Disagree
   - ❑ Agree
   - ❑ Strongly agree

7. *If a group home for people with mental disabilities were to open up in my neighborhood, I would make them feel welcome.*
   - ❑ Strongly disagree
   - ❑ Disagree
   - ❑ Agree
   - ❑ Strongly agree

8. *When I hear a friend making a joke about someone's religion, I laugh along with everyone else.*
   - ❑ Strongly disagree
   - ❑ Disagree
   - ❑ Agree
   - ❑ Strongly agree

9. *You invite Kyoko, the shyest kid in school, to your middle school graduation party, even though lots of your friends think she's no fun at all.*
   - ❑ Strongly disagree
   - ❑ Disagree
   - ❑ Agree
   - ❑ Strongly agree

10. *You just found out that Sarah on your soccer team is HIV-positive (has the virus that causes AIDS). You no longer want to play.*
    - ❑ Strongly disagree
    - ❑ Disagree

- ☒ Agree
- ☐ Strongly agree

11. *Your closest friends come from a variety of different backgrounds in terms of race, religion, and beliefs.*
    - ☐ Strongly disagree
    - ☐ Disagree
    - ☒ Agree
    - ☐ Strongly agree

12. *You just heard that it will be very expensive to install ramps in your favorite restaurant. That means prices will rise, and your family will not be going there as often as they do now. You think, "Why can't people who use walkers and wheelchairs just go to another restaurant that already has ramps?"*
    - ☒ Strongly disagree
    - ☐ Disagree
    - ☐ Agree
    - ☐ Strongly agree

Scoring

For questions 2, 6, 7, 9, and 11, you get one point for each "Agree," two points for each "Strongly agree," –1 for each "Disagree," and –2 for each "Strongly disagree."

For questions 1, 3, 4, 5, 8, 10, and 12, you get one point for each "Disagree," two points for each "Strongly disagree," –1 point for each "Agree," and –2 points for each "Strongly agree." Add and subtract all your points to get your total score.

–24 to +2: Close-Minded. Open your mind and your heart by following these tips:

- Imagine how you would feel if you were the girl who was rejected by her peers. Think about what it feels like

Harriet Says:

When I was a young teen, I had a hard time dealing with the constant stares and whispers whenever I took my younger brother, Ian, for a walk outside. An injury to his brain before he was born resulted in severe mental retardation. While other four-year-olds could talk fluently, he could only grunt and use hand signals to communicate his needs. Those were the days when many people who were mentally retarded were kept out of sight. I loved Ian tremendously, and still do, but I remember feeling that in some way Ian's "condition" was a reflection on me—I was embarrassed and only let my closest friends even know that I had a brother at home who still couldn't speak. How much easier it would have been for me if people had been more understanding or if I could have shut out their cruelty.

to be unable to go to a restaurant just because you use a wheelchair. Are you angry? Hurt? Remember those feelings the next time you have an opportunity to exclude or include someone.

- Approach each new opportunity as an adventure, rather than with fear. Start with small steps, maybe by trying some food item you had never eaten before or by inviting an often-rejected classmate to a party at your house.
- Don't avoid people and situations because your misinformation tells you that you have reason to be afraid. Learn the facts so you can treat people without prejudice.

+3 to +12: On the Right Track. Now work on opening your mind even wider by following the tips described earlier.

+13 to +24: Open-Minded and Proud of It. Congratulations! Your job is to help your friends who are not as fair as you are.

Are You a *Humor Queen* or a Serious Princess?

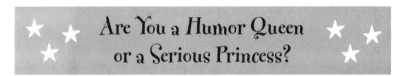

To find out where you stand on the continuum from Humor Queen to Serious Princess, decide whether each statement is true or false.

1. *When hanging out with your friends, you're more likely than they are to be the person who starts making jokes.*
   ☒ True ☐ False

2. *When they see the blank look on your face after they've told you something funny, your friends often need to remind you, "It's a joke."*
   ☐ True ☒ False

3. *At an awards ceremony, you'd more likely receive the Compassion Award than the Comic Award.*
   ☒ True ☐ False

4. *When your mom lets you choose one book to buy along with your school supplies for the new school year, you buy* 101 Back-to-School Jokes.
   ☐ True ☒ False

5. *Your teachers know you as the class clown at school, a reputation you probably deserve.*
   ☐ True ☒ False

6. *You would rather read the comics than the front page of the newspaper.*

   ☒ True ☐ False

7. *Your friends complain that you take life too seriously, especially when it comes to school.*

   ☐ True ☒ False

8. *Your agenda book for school is filled with all sorts of funny doodles and cartoons.*

   ☐ True ☒ False

9. *When you watch TV or go to the movies, you're more likely to pick a drama than a comedy.*

   ☒ True ☐ False

10. *If your school had a comedy show, you'd be the last person anyone would expect to sign up.*

   ☐ True ☒ False

Scoring

Add 1 point for every true answer on questions 1, 4, 5, 6, and 8, and 1 point for every false answer on questions 2, 3, 7, 9, and 10.

8–10 points: Humor Queen. You're always telling jokes and laughing. That is a good thing, but sometimes it can be too much for the people around you. You don't always have to be the class clown or family comic. Consider these points:

- Take a break from being everyone's comic relief every once in a while—it can get very tiring for you and for them. Stop thinking that the only way you'll be accepted is by being everyone's clown 24/7.

Liz Says:

I'm probably more of a "Serious Princess" than a "Humor Queen," but I can be funny if I want to and when I'm in the right mood. When I'm not in school, I love to have fun and joke around, but usually when I'm at school I'm very serious. My friends and I have millions of inside jokes that no one else understands. I even wrote a few of them on one of my textbook covers. One of the jokes is that you can always find a piano in Kristen's backpack. This is one of a group of jokes called the Four Sayings of the Prophet Zil (Liz spelled backward). The joke got started in either sixth or seventh grade while we were hanging around outside school and were seeing how heavy each person's backpack was. My friend Kristen's backpack was the heaviest of all of them, and everyone was asking her what she had in there that made it so heavy. Since she plays clarinet, I was going to say that her clarinet was in her backpack and that was why it was so heavy. But instead, I accidentally said that she probably had her piano in her backpack. And that's how the joke got started.

- Try being somewhat thoughtful when it comes to schoolwork, so your grades won't suffer.
- Sometimes having a friend who makes a joke out of every single situation can be annoying. Try to be serious when someone asks you to be, like when a friend has a distressing problem at home. A serious problem usually calls for a serious response.

4–7 points: Balanced Princess-Queen. You have found the right balance between humor and drama in your life. You know when and how to laugh, but you also recognize when a situation calls for some restraint. When you allow others to be the Humor Queen once in a while, you can sit back and enjoy the fun.

0–3 points: Serious Princess. You are too serious and rarely laugh. You need to lighten up and have some fun sometimes. Being serious all the time is hard work and can be very stressful. Here are some tips:

- Force yourself to watch a comedy movie or TV show instead of your usual drama. You might even end up liking it.
- Make time to have fun with your friends, instead of worrying about school and grades and family problems all the time. In fact, you'll be better able to cope with reality if you escape with a joke and a laugh now and then.

So you've started getting to know the real you. Like what you found out so far? If not, go back and look at the many tips scattered throughout this chapter. You can do something about many of your qualities, but perhaps it's more important to remember that it is your very uniqueness that makes you *you,* and nobody expects, wants, or needs you to be perfect. Keep in mind, too, that you will be changing a lot in the years ahead. Some of the characteristics that you're not in love with right now may be the very ones that will disappear or change in some way as you continue to grow up. Or you might decide that you really do like them after all.

CHAPTER 2

The Way You Really Feel

Are you sometimes puzzled by the way you react? Are you doing all you can to manage your stress, or does your life seem out of control sometimes? Is anger putting a dent in one or two or more of your relationships with friends and family? As you take the quizzes in this chapter, you'll discover the answers to these and other questions—a major step in learning to handle your changing emotional life.

How Do You Show Your Emotions?

Every girl shows her feelings in her own unique way. What's your special emotional style?

1. *When you found out that your friends were going skating, you asked to join them. They said, "Sure," and told you they would call you before they left. But when you got home from your music lesson and called, you discovered that they had already gone off without even leaving a message at your house. You:*

X a. get very angry and yell at your friends at school the next day.

___ b. go to your room and cry your eyes out. "Maybe they don't want to be friends with me anymore," you think.

___ c. pretend everything's all right and that you don't really care.

___ d. tell everyone around you for the next few days how mean your friends are.

2. *Your mom is supposed to take you to soccer practice, but she's twenty minutes late, and this is the third week in a row that this has happened. You:*

___ a. are so furious that when your mom finally arrives, you yell at her the whole way to the soccer field.

___ b. cry as you scrimmage, holding your head down and running fast so no one will see your tear-streaked face and start asking questions.

___ c. tell your mom it's fine, even though you feel rotten inside.

X d. explain to your coach and everyone on the team that it's your mom's fault that you're always late and complain to your teammates the whole time about how inconsiderate your mom is.

3. *You lent your friend Alison your favorite sweatshirt, but after four months of looking for it, she still hasn't found your shirt. You:*

___ a. yell at her for losing your shirt and vow never to talk to her again.

___ b. run to your room sobbing when you realize that you'll never see that shirt again.

X c. tell your friend that you can always get another one, even though you know you'll never be able to find one like it. (Your sister bought it for you on her trip to Italy two years ago.)

___ d. tell all your other friends how messy and careless Alison is and try to make them not want to be friends with her.

4. *You've finished your homework and your favorite TV show is almost on. But your dad says you can't watch it until you finish your English essay, even though the essay isn't due for another three days. You know that by the time you're done with the essay, the show will be over. You:*

___ a. scream at your dad and give him the silent treatment for the rest of the week.

X b. storm out of the room and cry about how unfair your dad is.

___ c. shrug and tell your dad. "It doesn't matter—it's just a TV show," although inside you're steaming mad.

___ d. run off to find your mom so you can tell her how unfair your dad is and how awful it is that you never get to see the TV shows you really like. Then you start working on your mom to agree with you, asking her to convince your dad to change his mind.

5. *You went to your friend's house on the weekend and ate dinner there. When you come back you realize, by looking at the pots and pans in the sink, that your family had your favorite meal: lasagna. You:*

___ a. confront your parents about it, saying, "You know that I love lasagna. You should have waited until tomorrow when I was home!"

___ b. cry as you finish your homework in your room.

X c. don't say anything and act as if you don't care and that you didn't even know they had your favorite meal.
___ d. complain to your brother about how your parents never make the foods you like when you're at home, only when you're away. Then you try to convince your brother that your parents do the same thing to him and that he should be angry with them, too.

6. *You worked really hard on a report for your science class. But, when you get it back, you see that you only got a B– on it even though you think you deserve an A, or at the very least a B+. You:*
___ a. get really mad at your teacher and slam your locker, abuse your schoolbooks, and stay in a bad mood for the rest of the day.
___ b. try not to tear up but end up crying into your pillow once you get home from school.
X c. tell your classmates when they ask that it was no big deal and you didn't work that hard on it anyway.
___ d. tell all your friends about how mean your teacher is, and you convince them that if they ever get stuck in her class, they should make sure they get transferred out immediately.

7. *You come home from school one day and are about to play with your hamster Annie for a little bit before you do your homework. As you're about to take Annie out of the cage, you realize that she's dead. You:*
___ a. yell at your brother when he gets home and blame him for not taking care of Annie.
X b. immediately start sobbing and stay sad for the rest of the week.
___ c. put Annie in a shoebox and bury her in your backyard. When your parents ask you if everything's okay, you tell them you're fine—it was just a hamster.

___ d. tell all your friends over and over about Annie's death and then get annoyed with them when they act as if they don't care as much as you do.

8. *You and your friend Stacy decide to meet at the skating rink on Saturday afternoon. You're not a great skater, but you were enjoying it until you lost your balance and pushed the little kid ahead of you down onto the ice. You:*

___ a. find Stacy so you can tell her what a stupid idea it was to go skating.

___ b. rush off the ice with tears streaming down your face.

_X_ c. apologize quickly and then continue as if nothing has happened.

___ d. tell Stacy that they shouldn't allow little kids to skate on that rink since they're always getting in everyone's way.

Scoring

Mostly *A*s: Raging Volcano. You tend to react to tough situations by blowing up. And when you're angry, you may say or do things that are hurtful to others and often unfair to them. What can you do the next time you're in a difficult spot? Keep your cool by reminding yourself not to react so quickly. Give yourself some time to get your feelings under control. Then talk to the person who set you off, and explain, as calmly as possible, why you're mad. Or just walk away—every situation doesn't require a conversation. Sometimes, the best course of action is doing nothing.

Mostly *B*s: Crybaby. You're not the type to confront others. Instead, you turn your anger or other strong feelings inside, where they become sadness and tears. You need to learn to talk to others about how you're feeling. It's okay to cry sometimes—in fact, it's

Liz Says:

I show my feelings in different ways depending on the situation. For example, I took this quiz and got every single letter answer at least once, but I got more Cs than anything else. I usually get mad and yell when I'm angry with my parents or brother. But if I'm mad at a friend, I usually keep it to myself but sometimes do talk it out with one of my other friends, who isn't involved. Sometimes I make things seem bigger than they really are, exaggerating to get my point across.

probably good to get some of those emotions out in the open, but you probably drag out those crying spells longer than needed, making mountains out of molehills. Remind yourself to put situations into perspective—one bad grade is not the end of the world; one stained sweatshirt does not destroy your entire wardrobe.

Mostly *C*s: Cover-Up Queen. Maybe you think you have to be Ms. Perfect with a perpetual happy attitude and a matching smile. You don't. Stop hiding your feelings and show the world the true you. Getting angry once in a while will not threaten your existence or end your friendships. You have just as much of a right to express yourself as anyone else. That doesn't mean that you have to throw dishes or shout curses. But keeping it all bottled up inside is not healthy, either.

Mostly *D*s: Blamer. When you're feeling bad, you want everyone else to feel lousy, too. And if you can blame something or someone else, you're happy to do that. Practice taking responsibility for both the things that go wrong and the things that go right in your life. Remember that just because something sad or disappointing happened to you, your friends and family do not have to share your exact emotions. Your misery may love company, but company may not want to get involved.

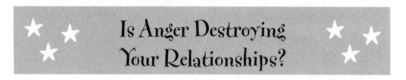

★ ★ ★ Is Anger Destroying Your Relationships? ★ ★ ★

It's normal to get angry once in a while, but is this emotion taking over your life? Indicate how angry you are likely to get in each of these situations.

1. *After you and your friend decide that 1 P.M. is a good meeting time, she shows up at the mall, out of breath, twenty minutes late, explaining that her dad had an urgent errand he had to run before dropping her off. You feel:*
   - ■ Not angry
   - ❑ A little annoyed
   - ❑ Angry
   - ❑ Red-hot furious

2. *Your four-year-old sister, who idolizes you and your stuff, gets just a little too close to your collection of glass figurines on your dresser and knocks one to the floor, shattering it. "It wasn't my fault," she sobs. You feel:*
   - ❑ Not angry
   - ❑ A little annoyed
   - ■ Angry
   - ❑ Red-hot furious

3. *Since you know the rule in you family is "No TV until all homework and chores are done," you start working right away when you come home from school. But today everything is taking longer than you expected. The show you really want to watch will be starting in five minutes, and you know you can't possibly complete everything in time. You ask your mom to make an exception, explaining that you'll finish immediately after the program ends. She says, "I understand, but you know the rule—the answer is no." You feel:*
   - ❑ Not angry
   - ■ A little annoyed
   - ❑ Angry
   - ❑ Red-hot furious

4. *The referee at your soccer game makes a penalty call on you for a hand ball that you didn't make, but just a few minutes earlier, the same referee failed to notice or penalize the player on the opposing team for making hand contact with the ball. You feel:*
   - ❑ Not angry
   - ■ A little annoyed
   - ❑ Angry
   - ❑ Red-hot furious

5. *When you get to the movie theater, you find out that the newspaper listing was incorrect. Instead of the sequel to your favorite movie, the theater is showing a thriller, which you've heard is truly awful. Now, it's too late to get to another theater. You feel:*
   - ■ Not angry
   - ❑ A little annoyed
   - ❑ Angry
   - ❑ Red-hot furious

6. *You feel that you deserve an A on the essay you wrote on sleep deprivation, a topic you know only too well. You spent a lot of time*

researching the facts, organizing your thoughts, and writing the paper. Not only do you get a B–, but other kids who spent far less time and effort received the same grade or higher. You feel:

❑ Not angry
■ A little annoyed
❑ Angry
❑ Red-hot furious

7. *A couple of your closest friends have been invited to a party that sounds like it will be lots of fun. You do not receive an invitation and tell your friends that, expecting that they will decline now. But they decide to go anyway. You feel:*

❑ Not angry
❑ A little annoyed
■ Angry
❑ Red-hot furious

8. *Your brother, who's just a couple of years older than you, has permission to stay out until 11:00 on Friday and Saturday nights. You think you're mature enough to have the same curfew, but your parents insist on 9:30 on weekend nights. You feel:*

■ Not angry
❑ A little annoyed
❑ Angry
❑ Red-hot furious

9. *You're standing on a very crowded bus when a sudden lurch causes the girl next to you to lose her balance, landing hard on your foot. The pain sends shockwaves through your body. You feel:*

■ Not angry
❑ A little annoyed
❑ Angry
❑ Red-hot furious

10. *When the notice goes up about auditions for the school play, several of your friends encourage you to try out to be the lead. It's something you've thought a lot about and really want to do. You spend hours in front of the mirror practicing for the part. But when the results of the audition are announced, you learn that not only did you not get the lead role, but you only landed the part of the most minor character, one who has only one line in the whole play. You feel:*
    - ■ Not angry
    - ☐ A little annoyed
    - ☐ Angry
    - ☐ Red-hot furious

Scoring

Each "Not angry" response: 0 points
Each "A little annoyed" response: 1 point
Each "Angry" response: 2 points
Each "Red-hot furious" response: 3 points

20–30 points: Full of Rage. Your anger is set off by everything, even when other emotions might be more appropriate. And the degree of your anger is probably often out of sync with the situation. If you don't learn to control some of your anger, you will lose friends, antagonize your family, and miss out on opportunities. Here are some tips:

- Figure out what specific situations are most likely to make you mad, and prepare for them with alternative actions. For example, if you know you hate it when you have to wait for a friend, let her know that you're only willing to wait five minutes and then you'll be leaving. Or bring something along to do—maybe a book or a sketchpad. Time passes very slowly when you're just waiting.

- Learn to put things into perspective. Yes, the movie you wanted to see is not playing at the local theater, as scheduled. Can you think of worse things that could happen? Of course you can. Try to remember that the next time you're ready to explode.
- Instead of fuming, which is not productive, do something. If you think your teacher graded you unfairly, appeal to have your test or report reviewed again. The important thing is to take action instead of stewing.
- Work off your anger with a jog, an aerobics session, a hard game of tennis, or some other strenuous physical activity.

Harriet Says:

I have a vivid memory of getting so angry—I have no idea what set me off—when I was five years old that I slammed the door to our china cabinet so hard that the glass shattered. As the years went by, I learned to control my temper and to channel my strong feelings into words and actions. Instead of just fuming about some injustice done to me or someone I care about, I articulate my concerns and state my opinions, whenever possible. Of course, I don't say anything when doing so would jeopardize my safety. And sometimes, I need to remind myself that a particular incident is not worth my anger.

10–19 points: Steamed . . . Sometimes. Unlike a person who is full of rage, your anger doesn't overwhelm your life. A show of anger means that you care deeply about someone or something—not a bad thing, right? But when your negative emotions begin to get out of control, practice some of the tips described earlier. Also, keep in mind that getting all steamed up doesn't necessarily make the anger go away. In fact, blowing up may actually increase your tension, rather than decrease it. It's far better to resolve the conflict that's the source of the anger.

0–9 points: Afraid of Anger. Displays of anger, and maybe even feelings of anger, scare you, so you stifle them. And if you're angry but don't let it show, no one will know there's a problem—unless they're mind readers. Are you afraid that the people you care about will love you less if you show anger from time to time? They won't! Don't keep your anger bottled up inside, or it might erupt as a massive explosion one day, and that would definitely not be a pretty sight.

Are You Managing Your Stress, or Is Stress Managing You?

Stress is part of everyone's life. How well do you handle the challenges and changes in your world? Find out right now, and if you've become overstressed, do something about it.

1. *On a typical school day morning, you feel:*
   ___ a. prepared to meet the day's challenges.
   X b. a little anxious about your social studies test—you probably could have studied a bit more.

___ c. totally overwhelmed—you can't find your shoes, your backpack, and the signed trip permission form that's due today.

2. *When you come home from school, you:*

___ a. don't know where to begin—you have a project due tomorrow and a major test the day afterward, and you haven't done any work on either of them yet.

X b. spend a few minutes unwinding with a snack and your favorite magazine before starting on your homework.

___ c. turn on the TV, and before you know it, two hours have flown by.

3. *When it comes to sleep, you:*

___ a. catch up on the hours you missed during the week by sleeping until at least noon on Saturday and Sunday.

___ b. can't seem to get enough—you're always feeling tired.

X c. try to stick to a regular bedtime and waking time, even on weekends.

4. *When your best friend asks you to join the new Community Action club at school, you:*

___ a. volunteer to become the president—what's one more when you're already an officer of three other clubs?

X b. think carefully about the other activities you're involved in before making a commitment to join.

___ c. can't even consider adding another activity to your packed schedule—you know that one more thing will push you over the edge.

5. *If someone who didn't know you came into your room, she'd:*
   ___ a. run out screaming—if she could find her way out over the mounds of clutter.
   ___ b. notice that you have a system for putting away your clothes, but you obviously haven't applied it yet to your books and papers.
   X c. be impressed at how organized your stuff is.

6. *At 10:00 on Sunday night, everyone knows that you'll be:*
   ___ a. writing in your journal—something you like to do before you turn off the lights.
   ___ b. scrambling to finish the science homework that's due on Monday, and hoping you'll be able to get to bed by midnight since you just remembered that you also have to revise the essay you wrote in school on Friday.
   X c. wondering where the weekend went—you never had a chance really to unwind.

7. *When you've had a fight with a family member, you:*
   ___ a. figure out a way the two of you can resolve the conflict.
   X b. can think of several people you can turn to for advice or just to listen to you.
   ___ c. get so upset you can't focus on anything else.

8. *Since you have a lot of different interests, but not nearly enough time to pursue all of them, you:*
   X a. set priorities to make sure you have time for the more important activities.
   ___ b. expect your parents to figure out what goes and what stays.
   ___ c. try to fit them all in anyway—it's just too hard to make decisions.

9. *During an average week, you feel stressed:*
   ___ a. every waking minute—actually, your nightmares probably mean that you're stressed while you're sleeping, too.
   _X_ b. at least once a day.
   ___ c. only on those days when your schedule is more hectic than usual.

10. *You think that "time to relax" is:*
   ___ a. wasted time—there's always something you can work on.
   _X_ b. something you should strive for every day.
   ___ c. possible only on weekends or during vacations.

Scoring

1. a: 1; b: 2; c: 3
2. a: 3; b: 1; c: 2
3. a: 2; b: 3; c: 1
4. a: 3; b: 1; c: 2
5. a: 3; b: 2; c: 1
6. a: 1; b: 3; c: 2
7. a: 1; b: 2; c: 3
8. a: 1; b: 3; c: 2
9. a: 3; b: 2; c: 1
10. a: 3; b: 1; c: 2

23–30 points: Totally Stressed Out. Find a way to eliminate some of the stress you're experiencing—it's not healthy physically or mentally. Try some of the ideas listed here:

- Identify the major sources of your stress—dig as deeply as you can. For example, it's not enough to point to school as a stress. Is a particular teacher treating you in a way that upsets you? Are you getting more homework now than you've ever had before? Are you too tired to concentrate in school because you're not getting enough sleep? Once you've pinpointed the cause, you can lay out a strategy to deal with it. If you're sleep deprived, set a reasonable bedtime, and stick with it. If homework is crushing you, do a better job of scheduling your after-school time.

- Allow yourself some downtime every day, not just when you're experiencing devastating stress. It doesn't have to be long—even a half-hour could work.
- Include a minimum of three exercise sessions in your weekly routine.
- Learn some relaxation techniques, such as deep-breathing exercises, for those times when you're feeling extremely tense.
- Take good care of your body: eat a nutritious diet and get enough sleep. If you're alert and energetic, you'll be able to cope better than if you face problems feeling run-down.
- Set priorities and learn to make effective use of your time. You don't have to say yes to every opportunity, and you can eliminate some activities that are no longer working for you. If you're taking music lessons just because they're part of your Monday routine, but you haven't shown any improvement in the past year and rarely practice, decide (perhaps with a parent's input) whether you should continue.

17–22 points: Stressed, but Managing. Your stress level is moderate, but you can probably reduce it even further by following some of the previous tips.

10–16 points: Coping Well. Congratulations! You obviously know how to take care of yourself. However, the true test of stress management is being able to cope when times get tough. Think about people who can support you when problems arise, and make a commitment to keeping the good coping habits you've already acquired.

Liz Says:

I get more stressed out than I'd like, mostly about schoolwork. Sometimes, I have lots of things to do and not enough time to do all of them. I usually get stressed out the most on Sundays when I realize that it's getting late in the day, and I haven't even started on my homework. Obviously, my time management skills need work. I also have been known to procrastinate, putting off stuff I don't really want to do, like a project that's going to take a lot of time. When I'm up late trying to finish my work, I don't get enough sleep, and then I feel tired and even more stressed the next day. Sound familiar?

One way that I deal with the pressure of having too much to do is by making a "to-do" list and a schedule for myself. If I'm stressed but I still have time to do things that I enjoy, I'll try to relax first and then do my work. I relax by reading, playing games, talking to my friends on the phone or hanging out with them, or going online to send an instant message or do some "window shopping." I've found that once I'm feeling a little more relaxed, I can do a better job on my schoolwork.

Are You *Happy* Enough?

Do you tend to look for the silver lining in clouds, or do you expect rain to cloud your days? Are you an "up" person others want to be around, or do you rely on friends to boost your mood? Here's your chance to find out.

1. *You tried out for the team but got cut at the finals. You:*
   ___ a. feel good that you made it that far.
   ___ b. are too depressed to go to school the next day.
   ✓ c. are disappointed, but you realize it's not the end of the world.

2. *On a typical day, how would you describe yourself?*
   ✓ a. happy on the outside, miserable inside.
   ___ b. in a good mood.
   ___ c. down in the dumps and wanting everyone around you to join you there.

3. *You don't have any homework this weekend and would love to spend some time with your friends, but they're all tied up with other stuff. You spend most of Saturday and Sunday:*
   ✓ a. figuring out what you can do to make sure this never happens again.
   ___ b. working on a hobby you've long neglected.
   ___ c. moping around feeling sorry for yourself.

4. *You've just spent an hour getting ready for the big school dance. When your parents compliment you, you think:*
   ✓ a. "I'm glad they noticed."
   ___ b. "They're probably feeling sorry for me—I look like such a loser."

___ c. "I wonder how my friends will react to my new look."

5. *Which of these questions are your friends most likely to ask you?*
   ___ a. "What put that grin on your face?"
   ✓ b. "Are you okay?"
   ___ c. "Are those tears in your eyes?"

6. *You've gotten a much lower grade in your social studies class than you had expected. You:*
   ___ a. feel too rotten to even study for the math test the next day.
   ✓ b. try to figure out what you did or didn't do so history won't repeat itself.
   ___ c. go around trying to find another student who did even worse so you'll feel better.

7. *You're known in your family as the:*
   ___ a. mood swinger.
   ___ b. optimist.
   ✓ c. pessimist.

8. *It's the first day of school. You feel:*
   ✓ a. like a nervous wreck.
   ___ b. totally excited.
   ___ c. ready, but a little anxious.

9. *Your crush finally noticed you in class today and sent a big smile in your direction. You:*
   ___ a. think he must have meant it for the cute girl who sits next to you.
   ✓ b. hope he'll still feel the same way tomorrow.
   ___ c. are totally thrilled. Who knows what will happen tomorrow?

10. *You tried out for a part in the school play, and the drama adviser is about to post the roles. You:*
    ___ a. expect to land a part but know that you'll survive if you don't.
    ✓ b. are afraid to hope for the best—you hate being disappointed.
    ___ c. know that you don't have a shot at even a walk-on—you've never been a winner and don't expect that life will change now.

Scoring

1. a: 3; b: 1; c: 2
2. a: 1; b: 3; c: 1
3. a: 2; b: 3; c: 1
4. a: 3; b: 1; c: 2
5. a: 3; b: 2; c: 1
6. a: 1; b: 3; c: 2
7. a: 2; b: 3; c: 1
8. a: 1; b: 3; c: 2
9. a: 1; b: 2; c: 3
10. a: 3; b: 2; c: 1

10–15 points: Dumps Dweller. You're unhappy a lot of the time, and may not even see any reason for changing your attitude. But if you keep focusing on what can go wrong, you're preventing any happiness from coming into your life. Open up those blinds and let some light in. How? Here are some tips:

- Stop thinking about happiness as an emotion you will feel when you're older, prettier, smarter, stronger, etc. Now is the time to start grabbing the good times.
- Use positive self-talk ("I am smart enough to do well" or "I'm just as good as my friends") to boost your flagging emotions. Your mood has nothing to gain from the

negative self-talk ("I'm a loser" or "Why should she want to be my friend?") you're probably used to.

- Give yourself a limited time to worry, to feel bad, to feel sorry for yourself. Self-pity can become a habit. Don't let it settle in. If you do poorly on a test, remind yourself that you'll have lots of others. If you don't get the part or make the team, you'll have other opportunities in the future.

Harriet Says:

As far back as I can remember, way before I earned my Ph.D. in psychology, people sought me out to help them with their problems. Like my mother, I was the kind of person who liked to counsel friends or encourage family members. I felt good when I could say or do something that would make a difference. While I was helping others cope with their troubles, I was dealing with some serious ones in my own family. My younger brother, who turned four when I entered my teenage years, was mentally retarded and hyperactive. It was not easy to deal with the realization that my baby brother, whom I loved so much, might never learn to talk. However, I learned that happiness was not unreachable, even when I was surrounded by chaos. I figured out how to create spaces in my life where I could have fun and laugh and be genuinely happy. Fortunately, that ability has stayed with me to this day.

- Seek out friends doing fun activities. That doesn't mean you need to abandon a friend who's going through a rough stretch, but remember that misery loves miserable company.
- Make a list right now of activities that you can turn to when the storm clouds hang on. And make a separate list of people you want to be around when it starts getting too cloudy in your life.
- Take action when you can to change something that is interfering with your happiness. Although you don't have control over lots of things and people (you can't change your relatives and maybe not your teacher, either), remember that you do have the ability to solve some problems (you could study more to boost your grades, for instance).

Note: Look out for depression. If sadness has begun to overwhelm you and you feel depressed much of the time, it may be time to seek out professional help. Let your parents know your feelings are too intense to deal with on your own. Talk to your doctor, a guidance counselor, or a social worker at school. It's not a sign of weakness to be asking for help—it's the first step in making happiness a part of your life.

16–23 points: Happy Sometimes. Your mood adjusts to changing circumstances. You're realistic about what you expect out of life and are prepared to deal with misfortune when it comes your way. You may take some time to deal with problems and disappointments, but for the most part you know how to shake the blues. You might need to remind yourself from time to time that happiness is in your hands, so you don't waste time waiting for it to appear.

24–30 points: Happy Girl. Maybe you were lucky enough to be born with the kind of temperament that allows you to swing with the punches, or you've decided that putting a positive spin on life works for you. In any case, you're the kind of person everyone wants to be around because happiness is as contagious as the common cold, and a lot more fun. You bounce back quickly when things don't go your way, but don't think that you have to be happy 24/7. When you face difficult situations (and they're bound to happen from time to time), don't be afraid to let your true emotions show through. Everyone's entitled to be in a bad mood once in a while.

What Embarrasses You Most?

Getting embarrassed is a big part of a young teen's life. What makes your face blush and burn? Rank each of these 10 situations from the one that would cause you the greatest embarrassment (rank 1) to the one that would be least embarrassing to you (rank 10). So, the second most embarrassing item would be ranked as 2; the third most embarrassing as 3; and so on. (Each answer will have a different number.) Get it?

1. *You spilled your purple grape juice on your white sweater at lunch, and you still have five class periods to go before you can leave school.*
   1 2 3 4 5 6 7 8 9 10
2. *Your ex–best-friend tells your crush that you're crazy about him, and you've never even smiled in his direction.*
   1 2 3 4 5 6 7 8 9 10

3. *Your mom comes looking for you at school after she's heard that a hurricane was expected. Unfortunately, she failed to listen to the rest of the news story—the storm is expected in a nearby state.*
   1 2 3 4 5 6 7 8 9 10

4. *You dig into your backpack to find your calculator but pull out a sanitary pad instead—right in front of your entire math class.*
   1 2 3 4 5 6 7 8 9 10

5. *You've just taken a shower, and you're walking to your room with just a towel wrapped around you when you run into your older brother's friend.*
   1 2 3 4 5 6 7 8 9 10

6. *You're hanging out with a couple of friends making fun of people who aren't around—except the person you just described as having a mouth like a horse is standing right behind you and heard every word.*
   1 2 3 4 5 6 7 8 9 10

7. *In gym class, you're climbing the ropes and are about three feet off the ground when you lose your grip and drop to the floor.*
   1 2 3 4 5 6 7 8 9 10

8. *A girl in your homeroom pushes the school bathroom door wide open while you're sitting on the toilet, with your pants down around your ankles. You were evidently too rushed to make sure the latch was all the way in.*
   1 2 3 4 5 6 7 8 9 10

9. *A bunch of your friends are over at your house, and your dad makes a fool of himself by telling a joke that probably hasn't been funny for about thirty years, and, to top it off, he can't even remember the punch line.*
   1 2 3 4 5 6 7 8 9 10

10. *You just had a major blowout with your best friend, who decides to take revenge on you by sharing a secret you told her in*

Liz Says:

Just recently, a friend and I had arranged to get together at 1:00 on a Saturday. She told me that she and her parents would pick me up, so I should be ready. We had planned this get-together about a week before, but I had not put it on any of my calendars. I was sure I would remember, and I did, at least until Friday night. But then Saturday came, and I was relaxing in my pajamas watching TV when my brother said: "Hey Liz, one of your friends is walking up our driveway." That's when I rushed to my room, remembering the plans we had made. I quickly got dressed and brushed my teeth while she waited at my front door and her parents sat in their car, waiting. I was too embarrassed to tell her that I had totally forgotten that we were supposed to get together, even when she said, "You really got up late today."

I've had more than enough embarrassing moments, and after each one of them, I ask myself, "Why does everything bad have to happen to me? [I have been known to get dramatic.] What will everyone think?" But after a few days no one besides me even remembers them. Embarrassing moments seem like the end of the world when they're happening, but they aren't too bad afterward. In short, don't cry or moan or groan over them—they don't last forever.

Harriet Says:

One of my most embarrassing moments as a teen came when I answered the telephone to hear someone say, "Harriet, it's your favorite cousin." I was so sure I recognized the voice that I didn't even hesitate before I answered, "Oh, hi, X." The silence that followed my greeting made me realize that I had made an unfortunate mistake. We went on to have a brief, awkward conversation—I couldn't wait to get off the phone. The cousin who called was probably as hurt as I was embarrassed, and neither of us ever mentioned that phone call again.

I've been in my share of embarrassing situations, but the truth is, they are only moments in my life, and not very important ones at that. When I look back at them, what I remember is the humor—the telling of embarrassing moments can be hysterically funny. But most of them just became faint, insignificant incidents.

the strictest confidence, the one about the old stuffed animal you have to hold onto to fall asleep.

(1) 2 3 4 5 6 7 8 9 10

Scoring

Statements 1 and 7 are about your appearance—how you look to the rest of the world; statements 2 and 5 are about your relationship with boys; statements 3 and 9 are about things your parents do; statements 4 and 8 are about your body; statements 6 and 10 are about your friendships and peer relationships.

Look at your highest-scoring items—the ones you scored as 1, 2, and 3. These describe the situations that are likely to cause your most intensely embarrassing moments. It's probably impossible to prepare yourself for those uncomfortable circumstances since the very nature of embarrassment is that you're taken by surprise. You didn't know the teacher was standing behind you; you didn't expect to fall flat on your face in front of your crush; you couldn't imagine your mom coming to school with an umbrella. What you can do is remind yourself that everyone gets into embarrassing situations sometimes, even the coolest people at school.

What should you do when embarrassment strikes? Try to stay calm, and remember that the people who are watching your embarrassing moment are probably thankful that they weren't the ones in it. That means that they're sympathetic to your plight. And while they might laugh for a moment or two, they'll forget about what happened long before you will. As soon as possible, think about what a great story a good embarrassing moment makes, one that you can repeat endlessly as you meet new people throughout your life.

While your feelings are likely to change from day to day, they're yours. You don't have to have the same emotional life as your friends or your family. The same situation that embarrasses you may not even get a reaction from your best friend. What makes you laugh might get a puzzled look from your mom. Recognizing and accepting your true feelings is important, but so is finding a way to manage your stress, keep your anger under control (which doesn't mean totally under wraps), and be happy—at least some of the time.

CHAPTER 3

A Style All Your Own

Are you a follow-the-pack kind of person or more of a let-me-lead-you type? Do you create your own fashion style or search the latest magazines to figure out what you should wear? How do you make buying decisions? Solve people problems? Manage your time? You'll discover your special style as you answer the questions in the following quizzes.

How Do You Deal with People Problems?

Do you confront people problems head-on, or do you look the other way? Are you willing to compromise, or do others have to bend to your will? Find out how well your style works.

1. *Your group is working on an antidrug project in health class. You just came up with an idea you consider brilliant. But Billy tells you, "It will never work." You:*
   ___ a. tell Billy that you'd like to try out your idea anyway.
   ___ b. quickly agree, saying "You're probably right."
   ___ c. suggest that you try out your idea first but consider other ideas as well.

___ d. yell at Billy, "You don't know what you're talking about!"

2. *Your mom asks you to come right home after school to baby-sit your little brother. You:*
   ___ a. remind your mom that you were planning to do homework with your friend.
   ___ b. say, "Okay," even though you had been looking forward to going ice skating with a group of friends.
   ___ c. ask if you can have a couple of friends baby-sit with you since you had been planning to hang out with them after school.
   ___ d. angrily respond that you're "the only one who has to rush home after school to take care of a bratty brother."

3. *The yearbook committee meeting has barely begun, and already Nicole is getting on your nerves, telling you exactly how to do your assignment. You:*
   ___ a. stand firm, letting her know that you have ideas you'd like to share.
   ___ b. agree to follow her suggestions, even though you're burning up inside.
   ___ c. say that you're happy to listen to her suggestions, but you have ideas you'd like to try out, too.
   ___ d. demand that Nicole listen to you or you're leaving the committee.

4. *You and your friends are hanging out after school on Friday afternoon trying to decide what to do that evening. Sarah suggests that you all go to see the latest thriller. You're definitely not the thriller type. You:*
   ___ a. say that there's a romantic comedy you'd prefer to see.

___ b. go along with Sarah's suggestion even though you know you'll be hiding under your coat throughout the movie.

___ c. suggest that you find another movie you might all like to see.

___ d. say, "Absolutely not. You have to be an idiot to want to see *that* movie."

5. *Your best friend Kim calls you one evening begging for a copy of your math homework. She tells you that she didn't understand the assignment and can't afford to get a zero for missed homework. "Just this once," she promises. You:*

___ a. tell her that you understand, but you don't feel right about having her copy your work.

___ b. agree to fax the completed assignment to her right away.

___ c. say that you can't give her your homework, but you'd be happy to explain anything she doesn't understand.

___ d. tell her she must be nuts if she thinks you're going to give away work that you spent hours doing.

6. *Your cousin, who was going to act as DJ at your party, calls you at the last minute to cancel. You:*

___ a. tell her how disappointed you are and that you wish she had told you earlier.

___ b. brightly say, "That's not a problem." But you're furious since you now have to scramble to come up with an alternate form of entertainment.

___ c. express your disappointment and ask her to help you find another DJ.

___ d. scream at her about how inconsiderate she is and how you'll never be able to trust her again.

7. *You're fed up with how your softball coach is always criticizing you for bad plays but never noticing when you play well. You:*
   ___ a. let her know that it bothers you that she's so critical of how you play.
   ___ b. don't say anything even though it's very distressing to be judged so harshly by someone you look up to.
   ___ c. tell her that you appreciate her suggestions but would appreciate it even more if she would sometimes compliment you when you hit or field well.
   ___ d. tell her that you don't want to hear one more word of criticism, throw down your bat, and storm off the field.

8. *After your friend tells your crush about your feelings for him, he tells you that he'd never go out with you and goes on to list a bunch of your qualities he doesn't like. You:*
   ___ a. tell him in a nice, but firm, tone that you didn't ask for his opinion about your personality and that you like yourself just fine.
   ___ b. say nothing, but you feel sick after hearing what he just told you.
   ___ c. tell him that he doesn't know you well enough to make that judgment, but perhaps he'd like to have an opportunity to find out what you're really like.
   ___ d. insist on telling him what you don't like about him, and you make sure that your list is twice as long and three times as nasty as his was.

Scoring

Mostly *A*s: Straight Shooter. You tell it as it is—firmly and honestly, but with a bit of tact thrown in for good measure. You care

Harriet Says:

Growing up, I was more of a *B* type than anything else. I used to replay scenes in my head, substituting the words I should have said for the ones I actually used. As I felt more self-confident, I learned that you hurt yourself when you let others step all over you with their mean comments. And if you don't state your own opinions, people will just assume that you're in agreement with them. As an adult, I still don't welcome confrontation, but when it's necessary to disagree, I do—most of the time. Fortunately, I'm not in any danger of becoming a *D* type, and I would never want to be. Unfortunately, I know people who are, and I wish they'd take this quiz so they could recognize that quality in themselves and do something about it!

about yourself, so it's important to set the record straight when you feel that you're being attacked. You're not afraid of confrontation, but, fortunately, you don't overdo it. Any drawbacks to this style? Well, you might feel compelled to react to every slight, even the tiny ones that could be left alone and weren't meant to hurt anyway. And you might work on not just confronting but coming up with alternatives that can help move a difficult situation forward. See some of the *C* answers for examples.

Mostly *B*s: Doormat. That description may hurt, but you can do something about it! That's the solution. You tend to react to people in a passive way, avoiding confrontation, even the mildest kind, at all costs. But what's the cost to you? Lowered self-esteem, probably. And regret—do you sometimes wish you could redo a scene to say something different? Now comes the hard part—learning to handle people in a way that allows you to hold your head up high. Here are some tips:

- Ask someone to role-play with you. Choose a close friend or a family member—someone's who's not going to laugh at you and can give you helpful pointers. Role-play responding honestly to people who constantly criticize or disappoint you or who must have it their way all the time. Then when a real situation arises, you're ready.
- Prepare a script—yes, like in the movies—that you can use when a person treats you poorly. Whether people are canceling at the last minute or ignoring your suggestions, figure out a way to voice your feelings and ideas. Using a memorized script might seem phony at first, but in time, your words will sound more natural, and you'll even be able to create instant comebacks. But be patient—this approach does take time.
- Remind yourself that you're too valuable to be treated so shabbily. Even if you're not able to respond appropriately right away, all is not lost. You can revisit a situation, saying something like "I thought about what you said, and even though I didn't say anything earlier, I want you to know that I have a different idea." Or you might say, "I was hurt when you said blah, blah, blah yesterday."

Mostly *C*s: Problem Solver. Not only are you able to respond honestly, but you are quick to come up with alternate actions that might meet everyone's needs. You know how to create win-win situations—the kind where everyone involved feels good about the outcome. Your self-esteem is strong, and you trust your ability to create worthwhile solutions. You can lead a group to greatness, but you're also a valuable team player.

Mostly *D*s: Bully. Do you realize how your actions are affecting others? And do you care? Maybe that's where the problem lies. You're not afraid of confrontation. In fact, you're quick to strike at anyone who doesn't go along with your agenda. Unless you learn to calm down and start treating people with respect, you're setting yourself up for lots of people problems in the future. No one wants to work with or be friends with a bully. Figure out where all your anger is coming from, and learn that there's a big difference between honest confrontation and plain old nastiness. If you need help doing this, see a school counselor or another adult who can guide you toward a more positive approach to dealing with others.

Are You a Leader or a Follower?

Do you have what it takes to lead, or are you more comfortable following the crowd? Find out about your leadership style with this quiz.

1. *The Web Design club is starting this week at school. You:*
   ___ a. expect to take a leadership role, even though you know very little about Web design. You figure you can count on others for their know-how.
   ___ b. probably will do what you always do as a club member: stay in the background for a couple of meetings until you figure out how you can best contribute your ideas. You have plenty of time to share what you know, and, in time, you will.

___ c. know that you can learn a lot from a club like this. You expect to sit back and take it all in.

2. *Your English teacher has divided your class up into five groups. Yours will be working on diseases of the eye. You wrote a paper on the topic last year,*
   ___ a. but don't remember much about it. You guess you'll be learning along with everyone else.
   ___ b. so you expect to lead the group.
   ___ c. so you should be able to make a significant contribution.

3. *Your friends are having trouble deciding what movie they want to see. You:*
   ___ a. offer your opinion but are not very forceful about it.
   ___ b. wait for the others to choose, figuring you'll go along with whatever they decide.
   ___ c. suggest that they take a vote.

4. *If you had a life in politics, you would want to become:*
   ___ a. president of the United States.
   ___ b. a member of the House of Representatives.
   ___ c. a member of a U.S. Senator's administrative staff.

5. *At school, you are best known as:*
   ___ a. a great friend.
   ___ b. a great leader.
   ___ c. a great student.

6. *When your family is making summer vacation plans, you:*
   ___ a. organize the pros and cons of each trip so everyone can make an informed decision.
   ___ b. yell out your first choice and hope everyone else will agree.

___ c. volunteer to get flyers about the place you really want to visit.

7. *Maybe you don't know what kind of career is in your future, but you know you:*
   ___ a. want to make a lot of money.
   ___ b. want to be in a position to influence other people.
   ___ c. want to work in a big company so you can meet lots of people.

8. *You're more comfortable when you:*
   ___ a. can play a role in making decisions.
   ___ b. can sit back and let others make decisions.
   ___ c. can lead the group to a decision, even when it's not one you originally wanted.

9. *People who know you well:*
   ___ a. like to have you on their team because you can get along with almost everyone.
   ___ b. realize you have the potential to be a leader.
   ___ c. know that you can be easily convinced if enough people have the same opinion.

10. *You and your friends have decided to do something for your community. You:*
   ___ a. all agree that it's best to have an adult in charge.
   ___ b. hope that one of them will come up with a good idea, since you'd really like to do something worthwhile.
   ___ c. suggest some ways to find out what's needed and how to get organized to be effective.

Scoring

1. a: 3; b: 2; c: 1
2. a: 1; b: 3; c: 2

3. a: 2; b: 1; c: 3
4. a: 3; b: 2; c: 1
5. a: 2; b: 3; c: 2
6. a: 3; b: 1; c: 2
7. a: 1; b: 3; c: 1
8. a: 2; b: 1; c: 3

Liz Says:

I can be a good leader, although I often avoid that role. I tend to let others lead unless I have to. But when I'm in a project group at school, I'm usually asked to lead the group—probably because other students recognize that I know how to organize people and work.

The first time I ever really led a group was in third grade. We had to do an oral and written report on Ghana, and my group of five chose me to be the leader. My group must have thought that since I was the leader, I would do all the work. Two of the boys in my group only talked about television shows and video games the whole time, and the other two kids in my group worked very slowly, if they worked at all. I spent a lot of time telling the others to do their part, which was a big surprise to them—and to me—because they thought that I was really quiet. I finally got them to work, and we got a pretty good grade on the report, but only because I had the courage to be a leader.

9. a: 2; b: 3; c: 1
10. a: 1; b: 1; c: 3

11–15 points: Follower. You allow yourself to sit on the sidelines too often. What can you do to become more of a leader? Here are some tips:

- Start using positive self-talk (for example, "I have good ideas" or "I can help this group make the right decision") to convince yourself that you have what it takes to be a leader. After a while, you'll begin to believe your words.
- Act like someone who has power—the power to influence others. How? Show your confidence (it's okay to fake a little if you need to), and support it with knowledge (get the facts).
- Watch people who are the kinds of leader you would like to be. Maybe that person is a teacher, a Girl Scout leader, a religious adviser, or one of your parents. Notice what they do and say. How do they convince, inspire, coach, and motivate others? Practice these new actions until they become more natural for you.

16–21: Leader, Sometimes. You show your leadership qualities in certain situations. If you want to, you can develop those skills even further by using a couple of the tips we just described. But being a follower some of the time is not a bad thing; without followers, no one could be a leader. People who direct projects need supportive team members who get the job done.

22–30: Strong Leader. You know how to communicate and motivate. You expect people to listen to you out of respect, not fear. While you are confident of your own ideas, you value and use the input of team members. You recognize that your way is not necessarily the best way every time. As a strong leader, you're a great role model for others. But you might want to take a break from your leadership role once in a while and give others a chance to demonstrate and improve their skills.

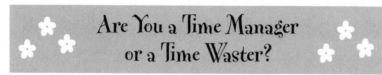

Are You a Time Manager or a Time Waster?

Time is very precious—no matter how you organize your day, you only have twenty-four hours. How do you deal with time? For each pair of statements, choose the one that best describes you or how you would act.

1. **A:** Before I go to sleep on school nights, I prepare my clothes and my lunch, and make sure my backpack is ready for me to grab in the morning.

   B: No matter how early I set my alarm on school mornings, I'm still scrambling to get my stuff into my backpack on my way out the door, and I almost never have time for breakfast.

2. **A:** I never seem to have enough time for all the things I want to do on the weekend.

   B: I set priorities and make time on the weekends for the activities I really enjoy.

3. **A:** I'm the cram-right-before-the-test kind of student.

   B: Knowing that I'm going to have a major test in a couple of weeks, I set up a schedule that allows me to study a little almost every day.

4. **A:** I always have to tell my friends that I'm too busy to see them on Sunday afternoon since that's when I first get started on my assignments due on Monday.

   B: I try to plan out my schoolwork so that I have some free time on Sunday afternoon—to unwind solo or hang out with friends.

5. **A:** Even though I'm still stuffed from Thanksgiving, I'm planning a major bash on New Year's Eve. I'll get started right away with a to-do list, and then delegate tasks to all of my friends with due dates for everything.

   B: During the first week of school, I had the fantastic idea of having a New Year's Eve celebration. Now, it's the last week of December, and I've barely started to call people—I know it's too late to send invitations even though I bought cool ones a couple of weeks ago.

6. **A:** "Where did the time go?" is what I ask myself at the end of almost every day.

   B: While I like to schedule some of my activities, I give myself room to take advantage of special opportunities that might arise on the spur of the moment.

7. **A:** When I'm invited to a friend's house for lunch or dinner, I usually get there pretty much on time. I think it's inconsiderate to be late.

   B: Even though I hate waiting for other people, I'm often late for appointments. Something always comes up at the last minute that prevents me from arriving on time.

8. **A:** I'd be lost without my agenda book.

   B: I write in my agenda book, but then I usually forget to check what's in there.

9. **A:** Procrastination could be my middle name.

   B: I've learned that putting off until tomorrow what I could do today is the formula for disaster, so I avoid procrastinating whenever I can.

10. **A:** I've lost credit on homework and school papers for handing them in late.

    B: I can't remember a time when I lost credit on homework or school papers for handing them in late.

Harriet Says:

If there were a gene for time management, I'd have it. My problem is not about time management—I'm one of those multitaskers who can read a book, watch television, and carry on a conversation at the same time. My problem is that I have so many interests that I hate turning down opportunities. I have been known to make a couple of appointments for the same time. The tool I have found most useful is writing down what I have to do and when I have to do it. I learned that through an embarrassing lesson. When I was in seventh grade, a girl named Leslie invited me to her party, and I was all set to go. The only trouble was I never wrote down the date and time. You know the rest of the story. One Saturday night my dad said the phone was for me, and as soon as I heard Leslie's voice, even before she said, "Where were you?" I knew exactly why she was calling.

Scoring:

Give yourself one point for each of the following: 1A, 2B, 3B, 4B, 5A, 6B, 7A, 8A, 9B, and 10B.

0–3 points: Time Waster. You're probably missing out on all kinds of opportunities, let alone fun times, because of your poor time management skills. Becoming more aware of how you spend your time will clue you in to where you're wasting it. Do this activity: Keep a time diary for a couple of days, writing in every single thing you do (yes, time in the bathroom does count), and then look at it honestly. Circle activities that you could spend less time on (perhaps you could take a four-minute shower instead of a fifteen-minute one—you'd conserve water, too), and cross out activities that you shouldn't have done at all (did you watch at least one truly lousy television show?). Use the results of your diary to make a commitment to change at least a couple of the ways you now use your time. If you don't seem to be making progress with those changes or you've set goals for yourself that are impossible to reach, review your diary once again. Figure out a different way to make better use of your time. If you do this exercise a few times over the course of a year, your new time management skills will begin to be a natural part of how you function. Don't waste any more time—get started right now!

4–6 points: Time Manager in Training. You evidently have developed some decent time management strategies. To be even more on top of your time, do the exercise described above. Sometimes, just tracking how you spend your day leads to changes—seeing really is believing.

7–10 points: Time Manager. You're at the top of the class in terms of time management. And you could probably give a couple of lessons to your friends. But don't become a slave to time—some unscheduled, unplanned time is not a bad thing. If you don't allow open time in your life, you might have to start worrying about managing the stress that comes with programming every last second of your day.

Are You a Savvy Consumer?

Is the mall one of your favorite hangouts, or do you shop only when you absolutely have to? Does the word *sale* make your heart beat wildly? And are you really knowledgeable about what makes a sale a real saver?

1. *At the end of a typical week, you've spent almost every penny of your allowance and earnings.*
   ❑ True ❑ False

2. *When you go to the mall, you often end up buying clothes that have been marked down, even if you don't really need them.*
   ❑ True ❑ False

3. *You save at least part of the money you earn so you can buy something really big and important later on.*
   ❑ True ❑ False

4. *When you go to the movies, you always buy a large popcorn and drink and candy.*
   ❑ True ❑ False

5. *Even though you don't have any more money than your friends, you're always treating them to snacks, movies, or whatever.*
   ❑ True ❑ False

6. *When buying snacks for a party, you buy in bulk to save money. You can always save the leftovers.*
   ❑ True ❑ False

7. *When you're planning on buying something expensive, you comparison shop, so you know you're getting the best deal.*
   ❑ True ❑ False

8. *You don't get an allowance—your parents give you money when you need it.*
   ❑ True ❑ False

9. *You've been known to forget about your plan to start saving for college as soon as your eyes spot a hot CD or trendy top.*
   ❑ True ❑ False

10. *You ask your friends to borrow money at least once a week.*
    ❑ True ❑ False

11. *When making a holiday wish list for the different members of your family, you divide up the list and make sure the gifts on each person's list are within their price range.*
    ❑ True ❑ False

12. *You have a 100 percent record—you've never made a budget and kept to it.*
    ❑ True ❑ False

13. *You've had so many advances on your allowance, you should be twenty-five years old now.*
    ❑ True ❑ False

14. *When there's something you really want, you don't mind splurging once in a while.*
    ❑ True ❑ False

15. *You know that all sales are not equal. Some are better bargains than others, so you keep your wits about you and look for items that really are super buys.*
❑ True ❑ False

Scoring

Score $1 for each of the following questions you answered as true: 3, 6, 7, 11, 14, and 15; score $1 for each of the following questions you answered as false: 1, 2, 4, 5, 8, 9, 10, 12, and 13.

$0–$5: Consumer Newbie. You have a lot to learn about saving and spending. Fortunately, you're at the right age to start those lessons. Here are some tips:

- Remember that a sale is only a bargain when you get something that has real value. If you buy a sweater in a color and style that you'll never wear just because it's been marked down three times, you're wasting rather than saving your money.
- If you don't already get an allowance, let your parents know that allowances are great learning tools—you can make and track a budget, and you can save up for something you really want.
- If you run out of money before the week's up, you frequently need an advance on your allowance, or your friends run before you get a chance to ask for a loan once again, take a long, hard look at your spending habits. Start by listing every single thing you buy for two weeks. Did you really need everything? Figure out what you can live without, at least some of the time. That way, when you need to save up for something really big, like college or a car, you'll already be in the habit of being a savvy consumer.

$6–$10: Aware Consumer. You're on the right track, but you need to work just a bit harder. A large popcorn, soda, and candy *every* single time you go to the movies? Try to do weekly or monthly budgeting and track where your money's going. Review the tips listed earlier. Seeing the facts in black and white can make the difference between someone who has enough for that special something and someone who's constantly playing catch-up.

$11–$15: Savvy Consumer. You know just what you have to do to stay on top of the money picture. You can recognize a real bargain, but you also allow yourself to splurge sometimes—when it's something that you really, really want. You don't allow money to control you but instead use it to make the most out of

Liz Says:

Since I was seven years old, I had other ways besides my allowance to make money. I used to create and sell jewelry—this started as my brother's business, which I bought from him. Then I went on to constructing clay miniatures. My customers were mainly people who worked at my mom's office. Now I earn extra money by baby-sitting. In fact, I have a regular baby-sitting job, which gives me a steady source of income and helps me feel mature and responsible. Of course, writing books is another way to make extra money, but almost all of that goes into a college fund. What is most important is that I really enjoy the work that I do, whether it's writing, making jewelry and miniatures, or baby-sitting. But I certainly don't mind earning the money!

life. One caution: Don't get so caught up in being a savvy consumer that you forget the joy that comes from giving to others or from buying things that are totally frivolous once in a while.

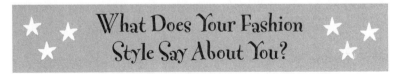

What Does Your Fashion Style Say About You?

Do your clothes tell the world you're a Trendsetter, a Who-Cares-Anyway Type, a Fashion Slave, or a Unique Stylist? Are you using your wardrobe to keep your identity a secret or to shout out who you are?

1. *You just got your favorite magazine and flipping through it, you find an article saying that plaid is going to be the next big fashion thing. You:*
   ___ a. immediately go to the mall and buy three pairs of plaid pants.
   ___ b. ignore the prediction and continue wearing denim every day. Who cares what the new look is? Jeans will never go out of style anyway, so why waste your money on clothes that'll go out of style in a few weeks?
   ___ c. wait until you see at least a half dozen other girls wearing plaid pants before you go out and buy a pair. If it doesn't end up being a trend, you've saved yourself from the embarrassment of being different.
   ___ d. get a plaid shirt to wear over a T-shirt.

2. *On Friday, you see one of the popular girls wearing a shirt that you think is really cool. You:*
   ___ a. decide to buy the same shirt but get it in red in a cropped length since you suspect that bright colors and short tops will be the hot trend this spring.

___ b. forget about it and keep on wearing the comfy flannel shirts you've always worn.

___ c. wait to see whether others will take on this new look. When you see five more girls wearing similar shirts on Monday, you decide that it's worth giving the new look a try.

___ d. decide that you like the pattern, but not on a shirt. A similar pattern on a scarf would work well for you.

3. *For your birthday you get a sweater from your cousin as a gift. Unfortunately, it isn't exactly in style. You:*

___ a. stuff it in the back of your closet and hope that your mom doesn't find it before it gets too small.

___ b. decide to wear it anyway. Who cares whether it's in style or not? You think it looks fine on you.

___ c. keep yourself on high fashion alert for the next week. When you see that no one wears anything like it, you tell your mom that it doesn't fit well and ask her if you can give it away.

___ d. try it on and realize that it actually looks okay but that it would look even better with a denim jacket over it.

4. *You're flipping through the channels and see your favorite celebrity wearing a really cool dress. You:*

___ a. go out and immediately buy a similar dress before anyone else gets hold of one.

___ b. tell yourself that it's not worth wasting the time and money to go out searching for a new dress, and you continue wearing the one you've always worn to parties.

___ c. find a similar one while you're out shopping with your friends but refuse to buy it unless someone else buys the same dress in a different color.

___ d. imagine yourself with the dress on and come to the conclusion that it wouldn't really look that good on you, so you don't put it on your shopping list.

5. *A week after you get a new shirt, you realize that it looked familiar because it was in style last year. Maybe that's why the head cheerleader rolled her eyes at you in homeroom this morning. You:*
   ___ a. "accidentally" shrink it so your mom will buy you a shirt that's actually in style.
   ___ b. continue wearing it. What does it matter what other people think? What matters is that it's comfortable and it was a bargain.
   ___ c. put it in the pile of clothes your family is donating to charity and hope your mom doesn't notice that your new shirt is in there.
   ___ d. wear it anyway since you think it looks really good on you.

6. *On a day when you're staying home and not seeing any friends, you wear*
   ___ a. the same stylish clothes that you wear when you do see other people.
   ___ b. a pair of baggy pants and a loose sweater.
   ___ c. an outfit that your mom made you keep and said you had to wear. But you wouldn't be caught dead wearing something that out of style to school.
   ___ d. several different outfits, experimenting with a variety of new looks.

7. *When you go to the hair stylist, you:*
   ___ a. show her a picture you found in a magazine of a model with a hairstyle that you really like.
   ___ b. just ask her to trim a few inches off the style you already have.

___ c. give her a photo of one of the popular girls. You've been waiting forever for your hair to grow out so you could have your hair cut like that.

___ d. ask for her opinion on a few hairstyles that you cut out of some magazines. You ask her which would look best with your kind of hair and the shape of your face.

8. *The big school dance is coming up next week, and you want to look your best for it. You:*

___ a. go out and buy a new dress that the host of a fashion cable show said was going to be the next new look.

___ b. wear your favorite skirt, but with a dressier top than you would usually wear with it.

___ c. search for hours in the mall for the perfect dress. It's just a coincidence that the one you buy happens to look almost identical to the dress one of the trendy girls wore to your friend's party a few weeks ago.

___ d. wear a really nice blouse you already own, but you buy a new skirt to go with it and spruce it up with a really pretty choker and a cool cardigan.

Scoring

Mostly *A*s: Trendsetter. You are always on top of news in the fashion world and all your clothes are in style. You can't stand to be the second to wear the latest trends. Many people follow your lead and look to you for new styles. That's great, but make sure you don't find yourself obsessing 24/7 about what to wear. And allow yourself to take a break from your fashion role once in a while—wearing sweats from time to time can be very relaxing.

Harriet Says:

Fashion has been one of my hobbies for a long time. I have my own unique style, and I enjoy putting colors, styles, and accessories together in ways that others might not think of. When I was in junior high, my family had very little money, so I relied on hand-me-downs. But I remember saving up my baby-sitting money so that I could buy something new, and I decided on a red corduroy jumper trimmed with black suede—yes, that was in style back then. My fashion icon was my Great-Aunt Lilly. Whether she was staying home or going out with her friends, she always looked good—her hair, her makeup, and her clothes were perfect, at least to me. I credit Aunt Lilly with the fact that whether I'm going on a business trip, staying home alone with my computer, or going out to a fancy restaurant with my husband, I try to look my best. It's not just for others—I do it for me.

Mostly *B*s: Who-Cares-Anyway Type. You don't care what people think about your clothes and fashion sense. As long as the clothes you wear are comfortable and you like them, you'll wear them. But your fashion personality might be misinterpreted by some who think your appearance says that you don't care about yourself. Although that isn't the case, is that the message you want to present to the world? Maybe you could take some time for beauty and fashion once in a while, still keeping true to yourself and your style. You might even find that fashion is a fun escape from the serious reality of everyday life.

Mostly *C*s: Fashion Slave. You want to be fashionable, but don't want to risk wearing something even remotely out of style, so you just follow the fashion crowd. If you want to seem more like your own person, try trusting your own judgment a bit more. Choose what you think looks attractive on you instead of simply copying what the popular girls are wearing. If you think wearing the same clothes that they're wearing will raise your popularity quotient, think again.

Mostly *D*s: Unique Stylist. You have your own unique style and use it to shout out who you are to the world. You care less about what others think and more about what you think. This mind-set shows your self-confidence. You wear styles that you like, and when you follow a trend, you're sure to make it your own.

You're at a great age for figuring out what your style is, how much you like it, and whether there are parts of it you want to change. Keep in mind that style is much more than fashion, although that's a part of the whole picture. If you like your style, terrific. But if you're not thrilled with all of it, you now have new tools for dealing with people, money, and time. Start using them!

CHAPTER 4

Body Basics

Do you consider yourself an expert? Well, you are in one very important subject—your body. You know more about your body than anyone else does, but you probably could learn still more about eating right and getting fit. But just knowing the facts is not enough. How do you treat your body? How do you feel about the way you look? These are questions you can answer as you take the quizzes in this chapter.

Are You Good to Your Body?

It's easy to take your body for granted, but the way you take care of it now may become a lifelong habit. So if you're not doing what you need to do, make some changes now to get your body care back on track.

1. *You know you should brush your teeth at least twice a day. You:*
   ___ a. do brush thoroughly every morning and every night except when you're so dead tired you're afraid you'd fall asleep with the toothbrush in your mouth.

___ b. brush every morning when you get up, but at night it's a "whenever I remember" thing, which means almost never.

___ c. often substitute a mint or a piece of gum for a thorough brushing.

2. *Like almost everyone else going through the puberty years, pimples have started sprouting up on your face. You:*

___ a. know you should keep your face clean, but most of the time, you just fall into bed too exhausted to wash off the accumulated dirt and oil.

___ b. do a thorough job of face cleansing when you see pimples, but when your face is clear, you don't bother.

___ c. wash your face morning and night, and you would never think of going to bed with makeup on.

3. *Your hair is pretty oily now that you've hit the preteen or early teen years. You:*

___ a. wash every day with a special oil-reducing shampoo to keep it looking its best.

___ b. shampoo whenever you know you're leaving your house, which means every school day, and usually on weekends.

___ c. don't have time to shampoo more than twice a week; the rest of the time, you keep a baseball cap on.

4. *Getting enough sleep is a big part of taking care of yourself. You:*

___ a. are just too busy to get to bed on time during the week, and when the weekend comes, well, that's the only time you get to hang out with friends. Sleep is just not one of your priorities.

___ b. get a solid eight hours on school days, but the weekends are another matter—you're lucky if you get six hours each night.

___ c. try hard to keep to a regular sleep schedule weekends and weekdays—one that allows you to feel alert during your waking hours.

5. *When you're tired during the day, you:*
   ___ a. grab a chocolate candy bar for some quick energy.
   ___ b. take a brisk walk to wake yourself up.
   ___ c. promise yourself you'll go to sleep early that night.

6. *You've heard that drinking six to eight glasses of water of day is a healthy habit. You:*
   ___ a. can't remember the last time you drank even half that much—unless soda counts.
   ___ b. drink only when you're thirsty, which means that you probably only take in about three or four glasses.
   ___ c. carry a bottle of water around with you and refill it often. Six to eight glasses is a fair estimate of what you probably drink on a daily basis, more when it's hot or when you've been exercising.

7. *When it's really cold out, you:*
   ___ a. still won't wear a hat—it would turn into a bad hair day immediately.
   ___ b. wear gloves and a hat—you'd rather stay warm than be cool (and cold).
   ___ c. might turn up your hood or stick your hands in your pocket.

8. *The mother of one of your friends picks up a bunch of kids from the ice-skating rink and says she'll drive you all over to the hot new snack place. She tells you all to pile into her car, even though there are five of you but only enough car seatbelts for four. You:*
   ___ a. tell her you can't go anywhere in a car without a seatbelt—it just isn't safe.

___ b. climb in—the ride will only last ten minutes. What could happen?

___ c. call your house to find out if someone else can come over to the rink to pick up a couple of kids.

9. *At your friend's party, one of the most popular kids takes out a cigarette and a lighter, asking if anyone would like to smoke with her. You:*

___ a. say, "No, thanks." You're not doing something that stupid to your body even if it might boost your chances of becoming popular.

___ b. hope everyone else will decline, so it will be easy for you to do so, too.

___ c. are curious and think that one cigarette can't hurt. Besides, that one cigarette might be your key to becoming part of the cool group at school.

10. *Your eye doctor has instructed you not to wear your new contact lenses more than twelve hours a day. You forgot that tonight's the dance at school, and you've already been wearing them for that amount of time. You:*

___ a. figure it won't hurt to wear them just this once for sixteen or seventeen hours.

___ b. take them out to rest your eyes for a couple of hours, and then pop them back in for the rest of the night.

___ c. know you look fine in your glasses, so you'll wear them tonight. No point in taking a chance with your eyesight for one dance.

Scoring

1. a: 3; b: 2; c: 1
2. a: 1; b: 2; c: 3
3. a: 3; b: 2; c: 1

4. a: 1; b; 2; c: 3
5. a: 1; b: 3; c: 2
6. a: 1; b: 2; c: 3
7. a: 1; b: 3; c: 2
8. a: 3; b: 1; c: 3
9. a: 3; b: 2; c: 1
10. a: 1; b: 2; c: 3

10–15 points: Body Slacker. Your body is sorely in need of a friend, and right now, you're definitely not it. Look at the answers where you received only one or two points, and decide what you can do differently—starting today. Your body will thank you in the years ahead. Where can you begin? Here are some tips:

- Create a checklist of actions you should take every day, and then start following them. At the end of a week, check out your pattern, and see where you've missed the mark. Were you too relaxed in the tooth-brushing

Liz Says:

I take pretty good care of my body, but sometimes I forget to do certain things that I need to do, particularly when I am really tired. I also realize that those habits I've had for a long time I'm very good about remembering, but those that I have only recently started, such as brushing my retainer or using special cleansers when my face breaks out, I sometimes forget.

department? Did you not get enough sleep on the weekend? Did you go to bed without first cleaning your face?

- Brainstorm a list of "absolute do's" and "absolute don'ts." One item for your first list: Always wear a seatbelt in the car, even if you're just riding three blocks. Accidents often happen when you least expect them. One item for your "don't" list: Don't smoke a cigarette because you'd like to be cool, because someone asked you to, or because you didn't know how to say "No, thanks."
- Imagine how much better you'd feel and look if you took better care of your body. Do whatever you need to do to turn that image into reality.

16–23 points: On the Right Track. You're evidently doing a lot of things right, so pinpoint the areas where you still need to improve. You might try a couple of the tips described above.

24–30 points: Body Buddy. You care enough about yourself to take care of your body. Stay on track, even when the going gets tough—lots of tests, a big fight with a friend, whatever. Remember that some rules are meant to be followed *always*—think seatbelts, no tobacco and alcohol. But other rules can be bent from time to time without dire consequences; for example, staying up very late or eating junk food once in a while will not harm you forever.

How Much Do You Know About Your Body?

Take this quiz to test your knowledge about how your body works and what actions you can take to keep it functioning in top form. Answer true or false for each statement. Then figure out how you can fill in the information gaps.

1. *A height spurt is often the first sign of puberty.*
   ❑ True ❑ False
2. *Drinking water before working out can be harmful since it can cause stomach cramps.*
   ❑ True ❑ False
3. *For most girls, one breast is exactly identical to her other breast.*
   ❑ True ❑ False
4. *Exercising combined with lowering your calorie intake is more effective as a weight loss technique than dieting alone.*
   ❑ True ❑ False
5. *When a girl gets her period for the first time, she has just entered puberty.*
   ❑ True ❑ False
6. *Even if you don't remember them, you spend part of every night's sleep dreaming.*
   ❑ True ❑ False
7. *In general, teen girls need more iron than teen boys do.*
   ❑ True ❑ False
8. *Middle-aged women need much more calcium than teenage girls.*
   ❑ True ❑ False
9. *A girl who is anorexic (anorexia is an eating disorder in which someone starves herself) usually has a realistic body image.*
   ❑ True ❑ False
10. *Head lice can be spread by sharing combs, hairbrushes, or hats.*
   ❑ True ❑ False

11. *Even one bottle of beer or one glass of wine can impair judgment.*
    ❑ True ❑ False

12. *Cigarettes contain nicotine, which is addictive.*
    ❑ True ❑ False

13. *If you use a sunscreen with an SPF of 15, you can spend hours in the sun without damaging your skin.*
    ❑ True ❑ False

14. *The oil glands in your skin are both more numerous and more active during the early teen years, so pimples are likely during this period of life.*
    ❑ True ❑ False

15. *Stretching before and after exercising is a way to prevent injury and increase your flexibility.*
    ❑ True ❑ False

Scoring

You get one point for answering true to questions 1, 4, 6, 7, 10, 11, 12, 14, and 15 and for answering false to questions 2, 3, 5, 8, 9, and 13.

0–5 points: Body Bumbler. When it comes to knowing your body, you're desperately in need of some quick help—a Body Basics 101 course. Read all the true statements carefully, and if you don't know why they're true, find a reliable source of information to help you learn the facts. The knowledge can be obtained from books or from a helpful person, perhaps a school nurse, a health education teacher, a parent, or an older sibling. As for the false statements, learn what's not true about them. Armed with your newfound information, you should feel more comfortable with your body, the way it's changing, and what you have to do to stay healthy and fit.

6–10 points: Body Aware. You know quite a bit, but it wouldn't hurt for you to fill in some of the gaps in your information storehouse. Look at the statements that you marked incorrectly, and get the facts. The more you know, the more prepared you'll be to face any future health challenges.

11–15 points: Body Brain. You're smart in the way the body works. The question for you is: Are you putting all your knowledge into practice? It's never enough just to know the facts

Harriet Says:

When my sister was ten (she's eighteen months older than me), my mother gave her a booklet that explained all about getting your period. Of course, my sister immediately shared the booklet with me, so I was well prepared years before I actually got my period for the first time. But my mother, who was very open about lots of things, seemed to be too embarrassed to discuss anything related to body changes, so I didn't ask many questions. I remember searching the dictionary and encyclopedia for clues about various body topics. I'm glad that my relationship with Liz is comfortable enough that she can come to me with her questions and concerns.

about eating healthfully and getting fit. You have to live them every day. But don't start to obsess about every little thing—a relaxed attitude can be beneficial, too.

What's Your Body Self-Esteem?

How comfortable do you feel with your body? Do you appreciate your fine points but still accept your flaws? Are you realistic about what you look like? Find out how your body self-esteem measures up by answering these questions.

1. *When you're changing for gym class, you:*
   ___ a. stretch out your shirt and contort your body—anything to be sure no one gets to see you in your underwear.
   ___ b. feel comfortable getting down to your underwear, but you don't want anyone to see you naked.
   ___ c. figure, "Hey, what's the big deal about being seen without any clothes on? We're all girls in here."

2. *When you check yourself out in the mirror, you say to yourself:*
   ___ a. "I like the way I look."
   ___ b. "If I would only lose twenty pounds or so, I'd be almost passable."
   ___ c. "I didn't have that pimple yesterday—maybe I should use something to cover it up."

3. *Your class is going on an end-of-year beach trip. You:*
   ___ a. figure that if you can keep your shorts on, you'll be fine.
   ___ b. make sure to bring your swimsuit since it's a really hot day, and you know you're going to want to swim in the lake.

___ c. ask your mom to write a note excusing you—no way you're going to be seen by the guys in your class wearing a swimsuit or even shorts.

4. *When the cute boy you have a crush on tells you that you look really good today, you:*
   ___ a. know he must want to borrow your math homework. Why else would he give you such a ridiculous compliment?
   ___ b. say, "Thank you," and feel really good that he noticed you.
   ___ c. are surprised that he would say that to you.

5. *If you could magically change how you look, you:*
   ___ a. would start from scratch—there's not much about your body you want to keep.
   ___ b. can think of a couple of things you would change, but basically you're pretty happy with your appearance.
   ___ c. would want to change four or five things and then you'd feel good about how you look.

6. *You exercise because you:*
   ___ a. know it's healthy, and besides, it makes you feel good and it's fun.
   ___ b. are afraid that if you don't, your body will look even worse than it does now.
   ___ c. would like to have a more buff look.

7. *If you had to name your favorite part of your body, you:*
   ___ a. wouldn't be able to answer—you really can't think of any that you like.
   ___ b. would admit your favorite as long as you didn't have to say it publicly.
   ___ c. would have a tough time choosing between a couple of top choices.

8. *List up to six parts of your body you really like:*

    ___ a. ______________________________

    ___ b. ______________________________

    ___ c. ______________________________

    ___ d. ______________________________

    ___ e. ______________________________

    ___ f. ______________________________

Scoring

1. a: 1; b: 2; c: 3
2. a: 3, b: 1; c: 2
3. a: 2; b: 3, c: 1
4. a: 1; b: 3, c: 2
5. a: 1; b: 3, c: 2
6. a: 3, b: 1; c: 2
7. a: 1; b: 2; c: 3
8. Give yourself one point for each body part you named. You get a bonus of two points if you listed six answers here.

7–12 points: "Poor Image" Prize Winner. You have your work cut out for you—you are far too critical about your body. That doesn't mean you have to love everything about the way you look. But your negative self-view is preventing you from having fun. Learn to give yourself some positive messages. Instead of saying, "My stomach's not flat enough," you might try saying, "I like the way dance has strengthened my leg muscles." Get it? Be a little more forgiving about your flaws and emphasize your strengths. And if you're not already exercising regularly, start a program now—with clearance from your doctor first. Working out helps you feel more comfortable with your body while it builds your self-confidence.

13–19 points: Body Realist. You recognize that you don't need to have the body of a model to like how you look. But if you are not totally thrilled with a particular feature—maybe you'd like

Liz Says:

Mostly, I like how I look, although there are a few things that I would like to change. I used to spend a lot of time thinking and complaining to myself about my appearance, but I rarely do that anymore. I feel that if some people don't try to get to know me because of the way I look (I'm short and I look younger than I am), it's their loss. I think that part of the reason that I am confident about my body is that I spend a lot of time dancing. I take three different dance classes, and they're lots of fun, even though I have to work hard stretching, leaping, bending, and twisting. But dance has helped me get to know my body better. I've learned how to do things, like isolating and moving particular body areas, that have shown me the power of my body. When my classes are over, I feel good, not just physically, but my mood is better, too. All the girls in my classes look different in many ways, but they don't let their body types get in the way of their enjoyment of dance. Seeing all different body types wearing skin-tight leotards and jazz pants has helped me become less self-conscious.

your arms to have more definition—learn some exercises that target that area. And keep to a regular program of exercise.

20–29 points: Body Proud. You are very comfortable with your body, and your self-confidence shows. You take your imperfections in stride—you know that everyone has some. And because your body self-esteem is so high, others see you as attractive, too.

How Fit Are You?

Are you as active as you were when you were a toddler and never ran out of energy? Is your level of fitness as important to you as your looks? It should be. Find out how you rate.

1. *When you climb up two flights of stairs, you:*
   ___ a. feel great, ready to climb the next two flights.
   ___ b. feel fine.
   ___ c. feel like you're about ninety years old.
   ___ d. think, "Who climbs up stairs? Find me an elevator!"

2. *When your gym class is doing aerobics, you:*
   ___ a. outlast most of the others.
   ___ b. can keep up the pace.
   ___ c. get tired before most of the others do.
   ___ d. are in the nurse's office trying to get excused from the heavy-duty exercises.

3. *When your school holds its annual assembly to distribute physical fitness awards, you:*
   ___ a. are confident you'll be receiving the top honor.
   ___ b. will probably receive one of the middle-level awards.
   ___ c. know you've made good progress since last year, but not enough to earn an award.

___ d. will be cheering for your friends—that's as active as you're likely to get.

4. *Your best friend suggests that the two of you run a 5K race for kids your age next month. You:*
   ___ a. regularly run longer distances with no problem, so you expect to finish barely breaking a sweat
   ___ b. know you have the endurance for races of that distance since you've been practicing for a couple of months now.
   ___ c. better increase your training to be ready for race day.
   ___ d. tell her she'd better find another partner, but you'd be happy to watch her run across the finish line.

5. *When your gym teacher asks you to reach for your toes while sitting with your legs straight out and together, you:*
   ___ a. show off a bit by reaching out beyond your feet, bringing your hands well beyond your toes.
   ___ b. are able to touch the tips of your toes with the tips of your fingers.
   ___ c. stretch as far as you can and make it to your ankles.
   ___ d. wonder aloud how this skill will help you land your dream job.

6. *You're staying at a vacation resort with your family and step inside the weight room. You:*
   ___ a. go over to the ten-pound weights—you know you won't have trouble lifting those.
   ___ b. try out the three- to five-pound weights—they're about what you can handle.
   ___ c. have just started weight training, so you'll stick to the one- and two-pound weights—no point in overdoing it.

___ d. head straight out again—you can't imagine what possessed you to enter in the first place.

7. *You know you should exercise at least three times a week. You:*
   ___ a. work out every single day even when you're feeling miserable.
   ___ b. try to do something that's physically challenging almost every day—a long walk at a quick pace, ten laps at the pool, or a jog around the park track.

Harriet Says:

When I was a young teen, I was not very fit. I rode my bicycle once in a while and walked home from school and to friends' houses. I can't remember any family member or teacher or doctor or friend encouraging me to challenge myself physically. I played basketball and volleyball in gym class because it was required, not because I liked those activities. And when I could avoid them, I did. Unfortunately, it took many years before I realized how good it feels to be fit. But once I learned that lesson, I made fitness a regular part of my life. Today, I leave work in the middle of a very hectic day to put in my hour at the gym. I use exercise videos and take hour-long walks with a friend on the weekend. When I'm too sick to work out, I look forward to getting back to the gym. And I'm very proud of the one trophy I've ever earned—for coming in fifth place in a 5K race in my age group several years ago (though I admit only about ten people in my age group ran that race).

___ c. made that your goal a month ago, and you've been successful for the most part keeping to it.

___ d. figure that you get as much exercise as you need walking in and out of stores at the mall and pacing while you talk on the phone to all your friends.

8. *You're about to work out one rainy Saturday morning at home when your friend asks you to come over to her house. You:*

___ a. tell her you'll be over when you're done with your one-hour *Tough Training* tape.

___ b. suggest that she come to your house instead for your special weekend workout—a combination you've created of aerobics, weight training, and stretches.

___ c. tell her that you'll be there right after your half-hour light aerobics session. You've only been exercising regularly for a few weeks, and you don't want to skip a planned workout unless absolutely necessary.

___ d. breathe a sigh of relief and let her know you'll be right there. What got into you, anyway, thinking exercising was a good way to start the weekend?

Scoring

Mostly *A*s: Ms. World Fitness. It's great that you're in terrific shape, but examine your life to make sure you are not becoming a fanatic about fitness so that you're ignoring other activities and interests. Pass on some of your enthusiasm and tips for working out to your friends and family members—they'll be grateful for both your company and your guidance.

Mostly *B*s: Silver Medal in Fitness Winner. You've figured out how to fit fitness into your life—no small accomplishment.

Keep working out as you get older, and you'll continue to reap the benefits of a fit lifestyle.

Mostly *C*s: Most Improved Fitness Trainee. You may not have been working out for very long, but you're probably already seeing some of the pluses from getting and staying fit. Keep your eye on your fitness goals, and don't let a bad day here or there discourage you. Everyone has those, and they pass. Remember that breaking records is not the point—increasing your stamina, strength, and flexibility is.

Mostly *D*s: Champion Excuse Maker. The only thing that you're a champion in is excuse making, and that's not a prize to make you proud. So, get up and start moving. Start slowly and don't overdo. Otherwise, you might be tempted to use some muscle strain as an excuse to stop. If you're out of shape, check with a doctor to make sure your new fitness regimen is okay. Try to find a fitness partner who can help to keep you motivated.

Are You a Food Fanatic?

Eating right means making healthy food choices and eating the right amount for your build and energy needs. Some girls, unfortunately, become obsessed with food, focusing on food in an unhealthy way. Find out about your relationship with food by answering true or false for each of these statements.

1. *I think about food most of my waking hours and often in my dreams, too.*

   ❑ True ❑ False

2. *I skip breakfast most mornings so I can eat whatever I want at night.*

   ❑ True ❑ False

3. *I almost never eat without first checking out the calorie content of the food.*

   ❑ True ❑ False

4. *From time to time, I go on a crash diet to fit into a particular outfit for a special occasion.*

   ❑ True ❑ False

5. *All my friends say I'm thin, but I think I'm overweight.*

   ❑ True ❑ False

6. *At least twice a week, I have trouble sleeping because either I'm so hungry or too stuffed.*

   ❑ True ❑ False

7. *I don't like to eat with other people around because they often make comments about how much or how little I've eaten.*

   ❑ True ❑ False

8. *I hide food sometimes and eat it when no one's watching me.*

   ❑ True ❑ False

9. *My diet consists of less than 10 percent fat.*

   ❑ True ❑ False

10. *The first thing I do when I'm stressed, angry, or worried is find something to eat.*

    ❑ True ❑ False

Scoring

Give yourself one point for each true answer.

0–2 points: Healthy Eater. You have a healthy relationship with food, and it's a normal part of your life. You enjoy eating, but you don't obsess about food.

3–5 points: Borderline Food Fanatic. You should evaluate your relationship with food—it's probably not as healthy as it could be. Do something about that now, before you develop some kind of eating disorder. Start by looking at your true answers, and discuss those answers with someone you trust. It may not be easy building a different kind of connection with food, but the result will be worth it—a lifetime of healthy eating.

6–10 points: Food Fanatic. You're in the danger zone—get help right away. Eating disorders are a real threat to your health. Someone with an eating problem might be overweight, underweight, or average weight. Compulsive overeaters are obsessed with food and binge often. Those who have anorexia eat so little that they are basically starving themselves. People who suffer from bulimia eat huge amounts of food but then force themselves to throw up (or they might exercise compulsively or use laxatives after they have binged). Your doctor can help you figure out whether you have an eating disorder, what your weight should be for someone with your body type, and what you should be eating. If your answers to this quiz lead you to suspect that you might have an eating disorder, don't put off talking to a parent and getting professional help. The sooner you do that, the faster you'll start developing a healthier relationship with food.

During your preteen and early teen years, your body is changing quickly. You don't need anyone to tell you that—just look at how often you have to get a bigger shoe size or need to

Liz Says:

I am definitely not a "Food Fanatic." The only kind of diet I've ever been on is one that allows me to increase the amounts of vitamins and minerals in the food I eat. I know how important calcium and iron are, particularly for girls my age, so I try to eat foods rich in those nutrients. The only food problem I have is that I do eat junk food sometimes. I don't worry about that since I seem to have fast metabolism and don't gain weight easily, and most of the time my diet is pretty healthy. Although being skinny may seem to many girls like an advantage, it isn't always. It's hard to find clothes that fit me well, particularly the sophisticated clothes my friends are wearing. I also feel weird whenever my friends talk about their weight because I don't want them to be envious of me. The other time that I'm usually embarrassed is when people pick me up off the ground. They always make some comment about me being so light and ask me how much I weigh. I'm not embarrassed about how much I weigh, but I'm afraid that some people will think that I have some sort of eating disorder, which I don't. I wish that people wouldn't care so much about how much they or anyone else weighs.

shampoo your hair. You're getting used to one set of changes when another makes its appearance. Developing eating, exercise, and cleansing routines that are good for you is a challenge for girls your age. And even harder is learning to accept your body—every inch of it. Use the ideas in this book and advice from other reliable sources—magazines and other books, health professionals, teachers, and parents—to lay a solid foundation of information and healthy habits you can follow or adapt to meet your particular needs as you get older.

CHAPTER 5

For Better or Worse—Your Family

Do they embarrass you often? Fight with you constantly? Can they count on you to do your fair share? Can they be trusted to stay away from your diary? Are you more like them than you'd like to admit? The quizzes in this chapter will let you explore the ups and downs of your family relationships. You might come away with some tips that will strengthen those important bonds.

How Involved Are Your Parents in Your Life?

Do your parents think that they have to be a part of everything in your life? Or do they take a totally hands-off approach to what you do and who you're with? Maybe they're somewhere in between. For each of the situations described here, decide how involved you think your parents are likely to be. How involved are your parents when they know that you are:

1. *choosing an outfit for the school dance on Friday night?*
   ❏ Too much ❏ Too little ❏ Just right

2. *receiving your report card?*
   ❏ Too much ❏ Too little ❏ Just right

3. *meeting a new friend at the ice-skating rink?*
   ❏ Too much ❏ Too little ❏ Just right

4. *invited to a sleepover party at the house of a girl from school, and they haven't met the family yet?*
   ❏ Too much ❏ Too little ❏ Just right

5. *deciding what clubs or teams you're going to be involved in at school this year?*
   ❏ Too much ❏ Too little ❏ Just right

6. *planning to go to the movies with a group that includes a few boys?*
   ❏ Too much ❏ Too little ❏ Just right

7. *working on a major report for school?*
   ❏ Too much ❏ Too little ❏ Just right

8. *thinking about getting contact lenses?*
   ❏ Too much ❏ Too little ❏ Just right

9. *deciding how to use your allowance this week?*
   ❏ Too much ❏ Too little ❏ Just right

10. *drawing up a list of guests for your birthday bash?*
    ❏ Too much ❏ Too little ❏ Just right

11. *choosing "just for fun" books at the library or a bookstore?*
    ❏ Too much ❏ Too little ❏ Just right

12. *deciding how to earn extra money so you can buy a CD by your favorite singer?*
❑ Too much ❑ Too little ❑ Just right

Scoring

Add up the number of "Too much," "Too little," and "Just right" responses.

Mostly "Too Much" Ratings. Often parents who are overly involved in their kids' lives are just interested in what's going on; they probably don't realize they've crossed the line into the

Liz Says:

I think that, in most cases, my parents are involved just enough in my life. In some situations, I'd rather have them not ask so many questions, but usually it's because they're just hitting a sensitive subject. I know my sixteen-year-old brother wishes that our parents were less involved in his life; he's very independent and doesn't like it when they ask him so many questions about everything. I think they have a hard time controlling their questioning because my mom's a psychologist and my dad's a lawyer—they probe as part of their jobs.

"Too much" category. This is a situation that calls for an open conversation, particularly about the items you scored as "Too much." What they perceive as interest, you view as interference. You may be asking yourself, "Don't they have their own lives to concern themselves with?" Yes, they do. But they're parents—they are most likely more interested in you than in anything else. Don't shut them out, but do explain that you're becoming more independent (a good thing!), and work with them to establish new rules for your relationship. Perhaps if you told them a little more before they asked, they wouldn't have to pry so much. But it's also okay to keep some of your thoughts and feelings off-limits to them.

Mostly "Too Little" Ratings. Lots of girls would probably say that they'd like to be in your situation, but you might prefer that your parents show more interest in your life. Either they're too busy with their own lives, or they think that a hands-off approach is what you want at this stage. It may be tough to have this talk, but you need to let them know how you feel about their parenting styles. They can't change if they don't know that a problem exists. Use the situations in this quiz to pinpoint the areas where you'd like your parents to get more involved. Think of yourself as a tutor for your parents.

Mostly "Just Right" Ratings. You are lucky that, from your perspective, your parents are involved to the right degree in your life. They evidently care enough about what you're doing in school, who your friends are, and what your interests are. Remember that if you want them more involved in certain situations and less involved in others, you have to provide them with that information. As your needs change, keep them in the know.

Which of Your Family's Values Mean the Most to You?

Some of your most deeply held values come straight from your mom or dad. Part of your job during these critical preteen and teen years is to establish what's really important to *you*. You're probably struggling to figure out what works for you and what doesn't at this point in your life. By answering the questions in this quiz, you'll start to recognize what's at the top—and the bottom—of *your* list of values.

1. *On your birthday, the activity you most look forward to is:*
   ___ a. celebrating with your family.
   ___ b. opening your presents.
   ___ c. having a party with your best friends.
   ___ d. wearing something new that will grab everyone's attention.
   ___ e. having an exciting adventure, like white-water rafting or downhill skiing.
   ___ f. sharing your special occasion with others and making sure that everyone's having a good time.

2. *Which New Year's resolution sounds most like one you'd make?*
   ___ a. I will be a more caring and responsible daughter and sister.
   ___ b. I will find a way to earn money so I can buy something really special.
   ___ c. I will be a better friend.
   ___ d. I will take better care of my complexion and work out regularly so I'll look even better than I do now.

___ e. I will learn at least two new high-adventure skills—maybe snowboarding and rock climbing.
___ f. I will donate some of my time and money to help those who have less than I do.

3. *You're home from camp, and school doesn't start for another two weeks. What do you most want to do?*
   ___ a. go on a vacation with my family—we never have enough time to be together.
   ___ b. baby-sit as much as possible—this is a great way to earn money.
   ___ c. hang out with my friends day and night.
   ___ d. go through my closet and dresser and get rid of those clothes that are just not flattering anymore.
   ___ e. visit an amusement park and go on the scariest rides.
   ___ f. take care of abandoned animals at the local shelter.

4. *The career that sounds most attractive to you right now is:*
   ___ a. working with your family in a business that interests all of you.
   ___ b. investment banking—you've heard people make lots of money in that job.
   ___ c. one that allows you to spend time teaming up with others—connecting with others is a "must," whatever you do.
   ___ d. fitness trainer or stylist—you already know a lot about what it takes to look good.
   ___ e. leading trips through exotic places.
   ___ f. running a day care center for children with disabilities.

5. *Your English teacher asks you to write a paper on a topic that you care a lot about. You decide to write about:*
   ___ a. your favorite relative.
   ___ b. what you would do if you won a million dollars.

___ c. the ingredients of a great friendship.
___ d. the coolest looks for girls your age.
___ e. a fantasy trip around the world.
___ f. how one person can make a difference in her community.

6. *You're leafing through the magazine that arrived in the mail today. Which article catches your eye first?*
___ a. "Get Along Better with Your Sibs"
___ b. "Start a Business That Will Make You Rich"
___ c. "Grade Your Friendships"
___ d. "Makeovers That Really Work"
___ e. "Face to Face with Danger!"
___ f. "Girls Who Think Globally, Act Locally"

7. *Your neatly wrapped holiday presents are stacked up in front of you. You hope one of them will be:*
___ a. a new board game your family can play together.
___ b. cold hard cash.
___ c. a pair of movie tickets for you and your best friend.
___ d. a box of the latest makeup.
___ e. hiking boots for the high-adventure trip you're going on this summer.
___ f. a certificate that shows that you've adopted a whale, goat, or heifer for a village in Bolivia.

8. *If the people who know you best had to give you a nickname, it would be:*
___ a. Family Fan
___ b. Money Honey
___ c. Best Bud
___ d. Miss Teen
___ e. Adventure Girl
___ f. Care Bear

Scoring

Not every value is included in this quiz, but you can find out how you rank family, money, friends, appearance, adventure, and caring in your life. Other values that might be important to you are achievement, fame, justice, and peace. Can you think of some others?

Mostly *A*s: Family Fan. Your family ties are very tight, which is great. We bet your parents and sibs are grateful for your attention, love, and loyalty. Use the strong sense of security that comes from those airtight bonds to start venturing out. You won't be turning your back on your family, just broadening your world.

Mostly *B*s: Money Honey. You and money are like a magnet and a piece of metal—you can't resist thinking about it, earning it, and maybe spending it. Nothing's wrong with focusing on material things, but make sure you're still open to the rewards that come from other values, such as caring friendships and fun-filled adventures.

Mostly *C*s: Best Bud. You're a blue-ribbon friend. Those who have been chosen to be your pals are lucky, indeed—hopefully they are also loyal, caring, and helpful to you. Some words of caution for someone who values friendship so much: Be sure to still follow your own passions sometimes. You can continue to be a great friend while pursuing hobbies or activities that don't coincide with your friends' interests.

Mostly *D*s: Miss Teen. How you look has you hooked, which is not at all unusual at your age. But if you are constantly preoccupied by your appearance, you might not be aware that people are attracted to those who are fun, easy to talk to, and kind. Looks are just one ingredient in your life. Focus on all of your qualities, and others will, too.

Harriet Says:

At this time in my life, I'd say that above all else, I'm a "Family Fan." But I care intensely about other areas of my life as well. As far back as I can remember, it was important for me to achieve, whether it was in school or elsewhere. And it still is. Being recognized by others for those achievements means a lot to me, too. Friendships have always been vital to my well-being. I can't imagine what I'd do without the long walks and dinners with friends—more to catch up than for the exercise or the food. E-mail exchanges with friends are a form of therapy for me rather than a simple sharing of information. The biggest problem for me is that I care deeply about lots of things and many people, so making choices is hard.

Mostly *E*s: Adventure Girl. Excitement is your middle name. You're ready for adventure whenever the occasion arises. Your courage to try the unknown is admirable, but once in a while, you might want to relax with a true friend or hang out in a comfortable place.

Mostly *F*s: Care Bear. Your community, your friends, and your family are lucky to have you in their lives. You are a compassionate, supportive person who's going to make a difference in the world someday. Just be sure to keep a piece of yourself for you—you deserve some of that attention, too.

Do Your Parents Respect Your Privacy?

Privacy is all-important at your age. Do you have parents who totally respect your need for privacy, or do they want to know more about your life than they know about their own? Find out where they stand.

1. *Your parents want to come into your room, but the door is closed. They:*
   ___ a. open the door and barge right in.
   ___ b. knock and wait for your reply before entering.
   ✓___ c. knock, but before you have a chance to respond, they enter your room.

2. *You threw out some diary pages you had written a few years ago thinking that no one would find them in the garbage, but your mom noticed them when she was taking out the trash. She then:*
   ___ a. ripped up the pages so your brother couldn't read them.
   ___ b. took the pages out of the garbage and pored over every detail, laughing right in front of your face about the guy you had a crush on!
   ✓___ c. asked you if there were any pages that she could read and keep as memorabilia to show what you were like when you were younger.

3. *If your parents thought you were hiding something important from them, they would:*
   ✓___ a. tell you that you can always talk to them about anything, but other than that, they would leave you alone.
   ___ b. persistently ask you if there was anything you wanted to tell them.

___ c. search through your room when you weren't home and, on top of that, ask your sister to spy on you and report back to them.

4. *If your parents accidentally picked up the phone and heard you talking with your friend on the other end, they would:*
   ___ a. hang up right away—no matter how curious they were.
   ___ b. listen to your whole conversation.
   ✓ c. listen for a little while, but then hang up because they know they shouldn't eavesdrop on you.

5. *You seem to keep your bedroom door closed a lot of the time now. Your parents would:*
   ___ a. tell you that they really don't like your door closed so much—it makes them uncomfortable.
   ___ b. make a rule that you can't keep your door closed for more than an hour at a time, unless you're sleeping.
   ✓ c. do nothing—they figure that there must be a good reason for you to keep your door closed so much of the time.

6. *You've been writing in your journal for years, revealing your deepest thoughts and feelings. Usually, you keep the book hidden in the bottom of a dresser drawer, but one morning you're in a rush getting out of the house and accidentally leave it right on top of your desk. Your mom notices it when she brings a basket of laundry into your room. She:*
   ___ a. will probably read at least a part of it—you know she's been dying to know what you've been writing all this time.
   ✓ b. respects your right to keep your thoughts to yourself and doesn't even open it.

___ c. will read every last word and then repeat to your dad whatever she can remember.

7. *Your parents know that sometimes you confide in your older sister. When you're not around, they:*
   ___ a. gently ask your sister if she'd share what you've told her.
   ___ b. don't ask her anything—asking one of their children to betray their other child's confidence is just not their style.
   _✓_ c. probe until they get at least a hint of what's going on in your life.

8. *You've been instant messaging a couple of friends when the phone rings. Your dad answers and says it's for you. You walk away from the computer in the den and go into the kitchen to pick up the phone. Your dad:*
   ___ a. immediately goes over to the computer to scroll through all of your instant messages.
   _✓_ b. goes back to whatever he was doing before the phone rang.
   ___ c. glances quickly at what's on the screen.

Scoring

1. a: 1; b: 3; c: 2
2. a: 3; b: 1; c: 2
3. a: 3; b: 2; c: 1
4. a: 3; b: 1; c: 2
5. a: 2; b: 1; c: 3
6. a: 2; b: 3; c: 1

7. a: 2; b: 3; c: 1
8. a: 1; b: 3; c: 2

8–11 points: Prying Parents. Either keep everything you'd like to remain confidential under lock and key, or gear up to have a hard discussion with your parents about your increasing need for privacy as you're getting older. Perhaps you and your parents can work out an agreement that reflects both your need for privacy and their need to make sure you're not doing anything that may be unsafe. You might even write out a "contract" that describes appropriate and inappropriate behaviors on both sides. For example, your parents might agree to enter your room only with your permission, and you might agree to inform them about where you're going and whom you're going to be with

Liz Says:

My parents respect my privacy on different levels, depending on the situation. Sometimes my parents don't even realize that they are invading my privacy. For example, at times my dad thinks that because he can't hear me answer when he knocks on my bedroom door, it's okay to come in, and he doesn't need to knock on the door again. But usually they know what is crossing the line and what not to do. And if they do something that I think isn't giving me enough privacy, I tell them, and they stop.

when you go out at night. You might also ask yourself whether you're doing anything that's making it difficult for your parents to trust you.

12–16 points: Curious Parents. Perhaps your parents are curious about what's going on in your life because you confide in them less than you used to. And they're probably having a hard time recognizing that you're not their little girl anymore. Look for an opportunity for an open, honest conversation in which you and your parents work out a compromise that respects your privacy as well as their interest in keeping you safe. Help them understand your perspective, and try to understand theirs.

17–24 points: Respectful Parents. Your friends probably are envious that you have such trusting parents. But give yourself some credit, too—maybe your actions and attitudes encourage them to trust you.

Is Sibling Rivalry Tearing Your Family Apart?

Note: If you don't have a brother or sister, you can skip this quiz. But if you have a very close cousin or friend who spends a lot of time at your house, you might take this quiz with that person in mind.

A sibling can be your best friend or your worst enemy. And the very same person might be both at different times. Answer these questions about your relationship with the brother or sister who is closest in age to you; put his or her name in the blank space in each item. See whether rivalry or friendship is more typical in your family.

1. *When I have a problem at school, I am more likely to discuss it with:*
   ___ a. anyone but __________.
   ___ b. __________ more than anyone else.
   ___ c. a parent or teacher.

2. *On a typical day,* __________ *and I:*
   ___ a. have a serious fight at least five times.
   ___ b. argue strongly once or twice.
   ___ c. might have a minor disagreement, but not much more than that.

3. *My parents:*
   ___ a. usually treat __________ and me equally and fairly, and that's how it should be.
   ___ b. treat __________ as the favorite child in the family, and I resent that tremendously.
   ___ c. treat me as the favorite child in the family and, secretly, that makes me very happy.

4. __________ *and I:*
   ___ a. share a couple of interests.
   ___ b. are very similar in our tastes in music and clothing.
   ___ c. are as different as night and day.

5. *When* __________ *looks good, I:*
   ___ a. won't say anything—who needs an even more stuck-up sib?
   ___ b. might mention it if we're getting along okay at the time.
   ___ c. do not hesitate to say so.

6. *When I borrow something from __________, I:*
   ___ a. return it after he/she has nagged me repeatedly.
   ___ b. return it promptly and in good condition or replace it, if necessary.
   ___ c. take it without bothering to ask first—I don't want to take the chance that I'll be turned down, which is what usually happens.

7. *When a friend makes a nasty comment about __________, I:*
   ___ a. usually just ignore it.
   ___ b. stand up for __________. I don't like it when someone else says something negative about a member of my family.
   ___ c. tend to agree.

Harriet Says:

I'm one of four children, so I certainly know about sibling rivalry. But I've also experienced the kind of love and support perhaps only siblings can give. My sister Marsha is only eighteen months older than I am, so when we were both teens, we eagerly shared misinformation about growing up along with gossip about boys and teachers. Today, although our interests are very different, we're closer than ever.

8. *When it's __________'s birthday, I:*
   ___ a. need to be reminded to get a present.
   ___ b. try to ignore the day—__________ gets enough attention without more from me.
   ___ c. try to find a gift that will make the day very special.

9. *When __________ needs assistance with homework or a chore, I:*
   ___ a. will help out if I have the time.
   ___ b. try to make time to help out.
   ___ c. will only help if I'm forced to by my parents.

10. *At holiday time, __________ and I:*
   ___ a. stay out of each other's way as much as possible—who needs that extra tension?
   ___ b. enjoy our family traditions together.
   ___ c. spend some time together and try not to fight.

SCORING

1. a: 1; b: 3; c: 2
2. a: 1; b: 2; c: 3
3. a: 3; b: 1; c: 1
4. a: 2; b: 3; c: 1
5. a: 1; b: 2; c: 3
6. a: 2; b: 3; c: 1
7. a: 2; b: 3; c: 1
8. a: 2; b: 1; c: 3
9. a: 2; b: 3; c: 1
10. a: 1; b: 3; c: 2

10–15 points: Sour Sib. Your negative attitude toward your brother or sister is probably using up a lot of your energy.

Where does the rivalry stem from? If your parents constantly compare the two of you, that may be part of the reason. Or maybe you don't feel that you're getting enough attention from your parents. Whatever is going on, try one or more of these tips to boost a bond that's going to be around for a long time:

- The next time you're tempted to be nasty, imagine that your sib is a close friend, and act accordingly. You wouldn't treat your friend with disrespect. Why do so to a member of your family?
- When you hear your parents comparing you to your sibling, let your folks know that doing so is creating resentment and rivalry. It may be hard to speak up, but it will be worth it if you can get your parents to see how their behavior is hurting, not helping, your relationship.
- Go out of your way to find a common interest with your sibling, whether it's a TV program you both enjoy, a relative who annoys both of you, or a news event that's firing up the airwaves. Seek out an opportunity to discuss (not argue about) that topic.
- Focus on your sib's positive qualities, and praise her or his intelligence, courage, or sense of humor. Be honest—find something real and specific to compliment. You may be surprised by the positive reaction you'll get from an unexpected, no-strings-attached flattering remark.
- Turn to your sibling for advice on anything from boys to teachers. And, in turn, offer friendly, caring advice when you're asked.

16–20 points: So-So Sib. Your sibling bond is fairly solid but could probably use some bolstering. Try a tip or two from the list above. It wouldn't hurt you or your family situation to start strengthening a life-long tie. And typically, getting along is more fun than fighting.

21–30 points: Super Sib. You're evidently doing your part to create a strong connection with your sibling. Is your sib doing the same? A caring sibling relationship needs constant attention, and it can't be one-sided. If you're the only one being super, let your sib know in a gentle, nonthreatening way that you'd appreciate a change in behavior. Then be sure to notice and compliment the new behavior. It's easy to take family members for granted, but super siblings treat each other as if they're best friends.

Can Your Family Count on You?

No one likes doing chores, but someone has to do them. So to be fair, everyone in the family, except for the babies, should pitch in. Are you doing your share? For each pair of statements, choose the one that sounds most like you.

1. **A:** I make my bed without being reminded almost every day.

   B: Almost every day, I need at least a couple of reminders before I make my bed.

2. **A:** When my parents are really busy, I sometimes ask if they need my help.

   B: Even if I have nothing pressing that needs to get done, I wouldn't volunteer for any extra chores around the house—I value my free time too much.

3. **A:** I do my chores as quickly as possible, sometimes cutting corners, to lessen the time spent on them.

   B: Although I'm not thrilled about doing chores, I feel some sense of pride in doing them well.

4. **A:** When my parents are working late, I will prepare dinner for the family.

   B: When my parents are working late, I know which number to call for take-out food.

5. **A:** My room is typically a disaster area, with clothes, papers, and assorted unidentified objects strewn all around.

   B: Although I don't keep my room compulsively neat, I do try to keep my stuff off the floor, in the closet, and in dresser and desk drawers.

6. **A:** I know the difference between washing a load of delicate and permanent press clothing.

   B: Laundry is laundry—can't everything just be stuffed into the washing machine together?

7. **A:** When I'm asked to unpack groceries and put everything away, I know just where everything belongs.

   B: When someone asks me to get something from the pantry, I'm usually stumped. I don't put groceries away—how could I know where to find anything?

8. **A:** When I reach into the refrigerator to get out the pitcher of lemonade, I realize that there's barely enough for a small glass, so I prepare a full pitcher—enough for the whole family.

   B: When I reach into the refrigerator to get out the pitcher of lemonade, I realize that there's barely enough for a small glass, so I drink that. The rest of the family will have to find some other beverage to quench their thirst.

9. **A:** The houseplants have to be practically dead before I'd even notice that they need to be watered.

   B: I check the plants in my house at least once a week to see which ones need to be watered and pruned.

10. **A:** Even though I don't have an allergy to dust, I act like it so I don't have to spend any time in close proximity to either a vacuum cleaner or a dust cloth.

    B: While vacuuming and dusting are far from my favorite activities, I do them when necessary to keep our house looking clean.

Scoring

Give yourself one point for the following: 1A, 2A, 3B, 4A, 5B, 6A, 7A, 8A, 9B, and 10B.

0–4 points: Piglet. You may not care how your surroundings look, but some members of your family probably do, and you're evidently not doing your fair share. Instead of getting to household chores only when you're nagged, punished, yelled at, or threatened with being grounded, work some time into your daily schedule to get chores done. You're part of the family—it's time to start acting like a responsible member. To make these tasks almost pleasant, liven up your work with music. Or work out a time every weekend when your entire family can work together to get the chores done—misery does like company. Another strategy involves rotating chores among family members, so no one is stuck with the most dreaded chore week after week.

5–7 points: Miss Responsible. Maybe you need a reminder here and there, but for the most part, you take your responsibilities

Liz Says:

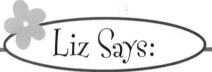

When I took this quiz, I ended up barely making it into the "Miss Responsible" category—my score was a 5. I thought I would be in that middle category, but not on the verge of being a "Piglet." It is true that sometimes I need to be reminded more than once to do my chores and that I rarely clean up my room thoroughly more than twice a month. Although I could write that I will try to become more responsible, the reality is that I probably won't change very much in this area—at least not right now.

as a family member seriously. Someday, when you're on your own, you'll be glad you learned how to prevent those jet black pants from turning your white underwear gray in the laundry, and you won't starve, either, since you'll know how to prepare a full, nutritious meal.

8–10 points: Mary Poppins. Your family depends on you, and you don't let them down. Even if they don't tell you, they're probably very grateful. But don't get too compulsive about chores—make sure you make time for all the fun things in life, too.

You may be spending less time with your family than you used to, but that doesn't mean you love or need them any less. It's just that your social world is expanding—and probably getting a lot more interesting. Remember that some of the changes your family sees in you may be scary to them. Think about your closed door, the secrets in your journal, your endless conversations with friends by e-mail and phone. To your family, these actions might be considered evidence that you are leaving them in the dust. Continue to connect and communicate with your family. Those ties with your parents and siblings can serve as a secure base as you become more and more independent.

CHAPTER 6

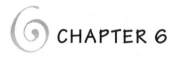

Friends 'til the End

Is popularity all it's cracked up to be? How far would you go to be part of the "in" crowd? Do your friends see you as cool? Are you a true friend, or do your friendships change depending on what's going on and who's around? You've probably noticed a shifting of your universe recently from the world revolving around your family to the world revolving around your friends. You'll discover more about that new focus as you take the quizzes in this chapter.

Are You a True Friend?

True friends are worth a lot more than their weight in gold. Do you have what it takes to meet the gold standard in friendship?

1. *Your best friend forever (BFF) just got a really great haircut. You love it and personally think that the style will soon be copied by everyone in the school. You:*

___ a. don't tell her anything. If you tell her what you really think, she might stop being friends with you and start hanging out with the popular kids.

___ b. compliment her enthusiastically, knowing that it'll make her day.

___ c. casually ask her if she just cut her hair and then tell her that she looks nice.

2. *One of your friends told you that she heard that your BFF cheated on the Spanish test she took a few days ago. You:*

___ a. tell some of your other friends what you've been told without first checking out the story with your BFF. After all, your BFF did tell you she didn't have enough time to study and that her mom would kill her if she didn't pass.

___ b. don't think that your BFF would cheat, but it is possible if she felt really pressured to do well on a test. Whatever actually happened, you're certainly not going to spread the gossip.

___ c. share the rumor with just one of your closest friends, and you ask her not to tell anyone since you don't know whether the information can be trusted.

3. *When your BFF asked you if you wanted to come over to her house and hang out, you said you were busy. You thought your parents were having guests over, but when that get-together didn't take place because your mom got sick, you ended up going to one of your other friends' houses for a sleepover instead. Your BFF is suspicious and asks you about your parents' party the next day. You:*

___ a. tell her that it ended up being canceled, but that's all you mention.

___ b. lie, and say that the party was really boring (so you don't have to say that you went somewhere else).

___ c. say that your parents' party ended up being canceled and that you went to another friend's sleepover party, but only because you thought that she had been invited, too, which was the truth.

4. *Your BFF has more friends than you have. She even has another friend who is almost as close to her as you are. You are a little bit jealous, so you:*

___ a. try to make a new friend who has the potential to become a BFF, but you still stay loyal to your original BFF.

___ b. admit to your BFF that you're jealous and that you wish that she had more time to spend with you.

___ c. decide to make your BFF your *ex*-BFF and lash out at her on the phone. (How would *she* feel if you did the same thing?)

5. *Lately your BFF has been saying she's really busy when you call and that she can't talk to you, but you know that you have much less time than she does, and you still find time to do stuff with her. You:*

___ a. start playing the same game when she calls, even exaggerating how busy you are.

___ b. don't try to fit her into your busy schedule (after all, she doesn't seem to be doing even that for you), but if it happens that you really aren't busy, you agree to spend time with her.

___ c. tell your BFF in a nice way that you feel hurt that she doesn't have time to be with you, but you don't accuse her of ignoring you.

6. *When you talk to your BFF on the phone, the person the conversation is about is:*
   ___ a. mostly you, but if she wants to talk about something in her life, you always listen.
   ___ b. almost totally about you. Most of the time when she brings up something that is about her, you change the subject or tell her you have to go.
   ___ c. equally you and her. You talk about what's going on in your life and ask for her opinions on problems. Then you listen when she talks about what's happening to her.

7. *You recently started becoming really close with a friend (almost BFF close). When your BFF does the same with another friend, you:*
   ___ a. write her a sharply worded note saying that if she wants to continue being your BFF, she should explain her behavior to you by the next day.
   ___ b. suggest that in the future when either of you do stuff with your new friends, you should try to include each other, too.
   ___ c. don't do anything. You understand that she has as much a right as you do to have more than one close friend.

8. *When your BFF tells you whom she likes and asks that you not tell anyone since you're the only person who knows (her cat doesn't count as a person), you:*
   ___ a. tell one close friend but admit to your BFF that you told one other friend—you know she'll find out anyway.
   ___ b. keep the information to yourself.

___ c. tell a few of your friends—the gossip was just too juicy to keep to yourself.

9. *Your BFF admits that she blamed you for missing her curfew on Friday night, even though you had nothing to do with it. But she says she's really sorry and that she's going to tell her mom the truth now. You:*
   ___ a. immediately forgive her—after all, she did admit what she did, and you didn't get into any trouble.
   ___ b. have a hard time forgiving her, but you're going to try.
   ___ c. tell her off. How could she be so selfish, blaming you for something she did wrong?

10. *Your BFF asks you to help her study for her social studies test at lunch. She says that she didn't have enough time to study last night, and she hadn't realized until just now that she didn't understand everything. You:*
    ___ a. tell her that you would be happy to help her study. After all, what are friends for? Besides, you can go outside during any other lunch period.
    ___ b. give her just five minutes—your time is very precious. You explain to her quickly what she doesn't understand and then go outside to hang out with your friends while she continues to study.
    ___ c. say that you promised to spend the lunch hour with one of your other friends and suggest that she find someone else to help her. Besides, you think that she should have studied the night before, instead of depending on you for assistance.

Scoring

1. a: 1; b: 3; c: 2
2. a: 1; b: 3; c: 2

3. a: 2; b: 1; c: 3
4. a: 2; b: 3; c: 1
5. a: 1; b: 2; c: 3
6. a: 2; b: 1; c: 3
7. a: 1; b: 2; c: 3
8. a: 2; b: 3; c: 1
9. a: 3; b: 2; c: 1
10. a: 3; b: 2; c: 1

10–15 points: False Friend. You are doing a great job impersonating a real friend, but you're as far from one as you can get. You have your work cut out for you if you really want to become a true friend. Here are some tips for you to follow:

- Allow your friends to be themselves. They shouldn't have to be your clones to be part of your life.
- Start giving your friends the attention and time they deserve—it can't always be about you.

Harriet Says:

It's easy to be a true friend when times are good. But when crises occur, people can tell who their true friends are. These kinds of friends listen to you as you describe, even cry over, your problems. You don't have to pretend to be cheerful just to keep them in a good mood. They encourage you to be your best, even when you have your doubts. True friends are not in competition with you—they want you to succeed. I think I am a true friend, but you'd have to ask my friends to find out for sure.

- Learn the meaning of some friendship words, like *trust, respect,* and *caring*. And then begin to put those words into action when you're hanging our with your friends.

16–21 points: Decent Friend. You have many of the friendship lessons down pat, but you need to work on some others. Look at those answers in which you received either one or two points, instead of three, and brainstorm some actions you might be able to take to become a better friend.

22–30 points: True Friend. You demonstrate the very best in your friendships. You're caring, forgiving, and trustworthy. Do your friends realize that you're a true gem? Don't let pretend friends take advantage of your A+ friendship qualities. Continue to be kind and giving to those who appreciate you, and expect them to do their share.

How Cool Are You?

You've heard of an IQ (Intelligence Quotient), right? Well, this quiz tests for your CQ, Coolness Quotient.

1. *It's the first day of the new school year. You:*

 ___ a. are wearing last year's trendiest clothes. Too bad you didn't realize until you entered the school building that they're now considered this year's bargain basement classics.

 ___ b. are wearing clothes that you feel great in, even though they may not be the latest fashion.

 ___ c. are wearing the hottest look around, and you know it.

2. *Your backpack sports the:*
   ___ a. school's logo. Too bad, your older sister told you that no one would be caught dead with that logo this year.
   ___ b. pins and key chains that give it that special "you" touch.
   ___ c. biggest name brand.

3. *The big dance is tonight. You:*
   ___ a. decide to wear the dress you wore as a bridesmaid in your cousin's wedding—pretty though not really dance material.
   ___ b. figure that the slinky black dress will give off just the right vibes, and you love the way it feels.
   ___ c. wear the outfit that just appeared on the cover of *Teen People*.

4. *Your school is holding a "What's Cool?" contest next week. You:*
   ___ a. spend hours in the library and on the Internet researching "Cool."
   ___ b. think that cool is a state of mind, and you're in the right one.
   ___ c. look through all the recent teen magazines so you'll know what to say, what to wear, and what to do.

5. *For you, the closest you can get to being cool is:*
   ___ a. copying the look that was popular last season—it takes you that long to know what's really "in."
   ___ b. doing and wearing stuff that feels cool to you—it doesn't really matter if others don't view them the same way.
   ___ c. being one of the first to be seen in the latest fashion trends.

6. *When you're asked to choose a school problem to analyze for a report and then design a solution, you decide to:*
   ___ a. study the weight of students' backpacks.
   ___ b. focus on teachers who are close-minded about any students who want to look at problems in creative ways.
   ___ c. study how unfashionable gym uniforms are.

7. *The kind of boy you think is cool is:*
   ___ a. the one all the girls are crazy about.
   ___ b. the one you can relate to because the two of you share a lot of interests.
   ___ c. the type who wears the hottest outfits.

8. *The walls of your room are covered with:*
   ___ a. posters of singers you're never heard of, but you've been told that teen girls are supposed to have rooms that look like that.
   ___ b. posters and artwork that you and your friends created to reflect each of your individual personalities and interests.
   ___ c. something different every month—it's hard to keep up with how quickly fads come and go.

Scoring

Mostly *A*s: Not quite cool, but trying. Evidently, you would like to be cool, but you're looking in the wrong places for the answers. Being intuitive about the latest trends is not exactly your greatest strength. Instead of trying so hard to figure out what's cool and then missing the mark, you might start looking at what makes you feel comfortable. You could also enlist the help of some good friends who can be honest with you about what works and what doesn't.

Mostly *B*s: True Blue. You're a one of-a-kind. Fortunately, you're secure enough to carry off your strong sense of who you are and where you're going. You know that being cool doesn't have to mean wearing the latest trends or hanging out with the most popular guys. Rather, your kind of cool comes from inside, and those who cross your path can smell your confidence a mile away.

Mostly *C*s: Cooler Than Cool. You're spending a lot of your time and energy keeping up your "Coolness Quotient." Is it really

Liz Says:

I think that I would pretty much fit into the "True Blue" category. I don't focus all of my energy on trying to be cool—I just do things that I want to do. I can think of people who fit perfectly into each of the other categories. I know one girl who isn't cool at all, but I didn't realize until recently that she was even trying to be cool. I noticed that she was actually wearing a pair of pants that were pretty cool. The only problem was that they were too small, rolled up, and very wrinkled. I have another friend who is "Cooler Than Cool." She is not the most popular person in my school, but she does wear all the latest fashions. She straightens her hair every morning and puts on more makeup than I would ever wear. I am not really like either of them. I wear clothes that I like and look good on me, and I decorate my room and backpack with things that show my interests and what I like, not what might appeal to someone else.

worth all that effort? And how good do you feel being so absolutely cool? Give yourself a break, and relax a little. You'll still be cool to your close friends, and aren't they the ones who truly count, after all?

How Far Would You Go to Be Popular?

Lots of girls want to be popular—are you one of them? How far would you go to attain this goal?

1. *You made plans with your BFF to go to a movie on Friday night. That was before you received the invitation that practically stopped your heart. A boy in your class who had barely talked to you before asked you to come to a party at his house to celebrate the success of the school's basketball team. You know that all the popular kids will be there. You:*
   ___ a. hope your BFF will understand that you have to change your plans. She would probably do the same thing to you. You tell her about the party you've been invited to and say that you'll get together with her later in the weekend.
   ___ b. make up a lame excuse about your parents needing you to stay home on Friday night. And then you go to the party.
   ___ c. would love to go, but you've already made plans for Friday night, so you decline the invitation to the party.
2. *Your nose is a little crooked or bigger than you'd like it to be. You:*
   ___ a. look at this feature as a piece of what makes you uniquely you.

___ b. ask your parents to find a surgeon who will make your nose look exactly like Miss Popularity at school.
___ c. hope that your looks won't hold you back from becoming popular.

3. *You have a limited spending budget. You:*
___ a. spend all of it on clothes and makeup that will allow you to copy the look of the popular kids at school.
___ b. use some of it for items like movie tickets and snacks, and the rest goes into the bank because you're saving for a CD player.
___ c. use some of it for clothes and hair stuff that will help you feel good about how you look.

4. *You are approached by a girl in your math class who is popular but not particularly smart. She asks if she can copy your homework, saying she was just too busy to do it herself. You:*
___ a. say, "Sorry, but I can't give it to you," with no further explanation.
___ b. lie and tell her that you didn't finish it yet, either.
___ c. hand it over to her without a moment's hesitation.

5. *One of the cool girls at school is working on a project with you at your house. She suggests using some of your family photographs for a collage. You know that your parents would definitely not be happy about your cutting up and pasting these pictures. You:*
___ a. agree to it anyway since you don't want the cool girl to think you're totally uncool.
___ b. tell her that you'll have to get your parent's permission first, since they can be so uncool about things like that.
___ c. explain that you'll have to complete the project in some other way since you know your parents wouldn't allow family photographs to be destroyed.

6. *To celebrate your mom's birthday, your family has plans to go to dinner at her all-time favorite restaurant on Saturday night. It just so happens that Miss Cool at school is having a birthday bash the very same night. You can't believe that you were invited. You:*
   ___ a. tell Miss Cool that while you'd love to join her, your mom's birthday is the very same day, and you've already promised that you'll be celebrating with your family.
   ___ b. say yes to Miss Cool and convince your family to have dinner at an earlier hour, and then you rush them through it so you'll get to the other birthday bash a little late.
   ___ c. tell your family that they'll have to come up with a different date for celebrating your mom's birthday since you have received a once-in-a-lifetime invitation to the birthday bash of the year and you absolutely can't miss it.

7. *A popular girl comes over to your house after school to see your new pet dog. The phone rings and it's your BFF. You:*
   ___ a. act like the caller is a cool boy who goes to another school. You really want to impress the popular girl.
   ___ b. invite her over, too. You don't want your BFF to feel left out.
   ___ c. rush your BFF off the phone since you don't want to waste the time of the popular girl.

8. *You're at a party in the school gym when one of the cool boys asks you to take a sip of some beer he smuggled into the building. You:*
   ___ a. figure it can't hurt to try it, and you know you'd get points for acting cool if you did.

___ b. pretend to take a sip so he won't think you're a nerd, but you make sure a drop doesn't touch your lips.
___ c. say, "No, thanks, I don't drink." If drinking beer is what it takes to be part of the cool crowd, you'd rather not be in it.

Scoring

1. a: 2; b: 1; c: 3
2. a: 3; b: 1; c: 2

Liz Says:

I'm not popular, and I don't intend to be if it means not being allowed to be myself. But to be honest, there is a part of me that would like to be popular. I would like others to look up to me and to think of me as someone who's cool and who does cool stuff. Adults think that writing a book, being smart, or acting nice can make you popular, but that's not true in the teen world. Most of those qualities make you a good person, a role model for younger kids, and a nice friend, but they don't lead to popularity. Often the things that do lead to popularity are superficial—good looks, great clothes, being the first to have or do the latest (whatever that might be). It all comes down to this: If I had to choose between being me or being popular, I'd definitely choose being ME!

3. a: 1; b: 3; c: 3
4. a: 3; b: 2; c: 1
5. a: 1; b: 2; c: 3
6. a: 3; b: 2; c: 1
7. a: 1; b: 3; c: 2
8. a: 1; b: 2; c: 3

8–11 points: Miss Popularity Wannabe. You would betray your real friends and family to be accepted by those who are popular.

Harriet Says:

Popularity has a whole different meaning in the adult world than it does in the teen world. Being popular for me now means being well liked and respected by a large number of people. With that definition, yes, I have finally achieved popularity. But as a teen, I was not part of the cool group at school. I was not willing to violate my own values or be cruel to others to win that role. I still remember one of the popular girls talking to her friend in my high school gym class about my "mousy brown hair" in contrast to her shiny dyed tresses. She intended for me to hear that cutting remark. I certainly didn't aspire to be like her. That doesn't mean that every girl who's ever been popular is mean. Many girls who are popular have lots of friends because they're generous and warm and fun to be with. That's the only kind of popularity contest worth winning.

Open your eyes to what's important in life before you lose those people who really should count.

12–17 points: Middle of the Roader. While you would like to be popular, you're not willing to take drastic action to achieve it. Remember that popularity is not all it's cracked up to be. Those who are popular now will not necessarily be the ones who are popular a year or even a month from now. And it's definitely not a guarantee of happiness.

18–24 points: Miss Confidence. You're mature far beyond your years. You know who you are and will not compromise your integrity to become a member of the "in" crowd.

Are Your Friends Right for You?

You've probably chosen your friends over the years for a million different reasons. Some of these relationships are still going strong, others are long-gone, and maybe some are still around but shouldn't be. Take some time to examine what works and what doesn't in your current friendship world. For each statement, decide whether you have a friend who fits that description; if you do, write down the name of the one who is guilty of each of these behaviors. See if a pattern emerges.

I have a friend who:

1. *makes me feel bad about myself. She's constantly putting down my looks, my clothes, even my family.*
   ❑ Yes ❑ No If Yes, who? ___________
2. *has tried to pressure me to smoke a cigarette or try a beer.*
   ❑ Yes ❑ No If Yes, who? ___________

3. *makes me feel that somehow I'm being disloyal when I get a grade that is better than hers.*
   ❑ Yes ❑ No If Yes, who? __________

4. *has asked me to lie to her parents so they won't find out about something that would get her into trouble.*
   ❑ Yes ❑ No If Yes, who? __________

5. *never gives me back the money she's borrowed from me.*
   ❑ Yes ❑ No If Yes, who? __________

6. *has pressured me to help her cheat on a test or do something else equally dishonest.*
   ❑ Yes ❑ No If Yes, who? __________

7. *always tells me my ideas stink no matter what I suggest.*
   ❑ Yes ❑ No If Yes, who? __________

8. *constantly forgets to meet me after she's made plans with me.*
   ❑ Yes ❑ No If Yes, who? __________

9. *calls me at the last minute to tell me that she can't see me—even though we already have plans—because someone from the more popular group has asked her to go somewhere.*
   ❑ Yes ❑ No If Yes, who? __________

10. *has a habit of criticizing my way of talking, giggling, or even just telling a story.*
    ❑ Yes ❑ No If Yes, who? __________

11. *complains when I make plans with another friend that do not include her.*
    ❑ Yes ❑ No If Yes, who? __________

12. *often blames me for things that are not my fault.*
    ❑ Yes ❑ No If Yes, who? __________

13. *acts like she's my best friend when no one else is there but tends to ignore me when other girls are around.*
❑ Yes ❑ No If Yes, who? __________

14. *takes big risks, such as staying out beyond her curfew and lying to her parents about where she's been. And to make matters worse, she won't listen to anyone's advice.*
❑ Yes ❑ No If Yes, who? __________

Scoring

How many yes answers did you give? More than five? That's certainly a warning sign about one or more of the people you hang around with. How many different friends did you mention? If each person fits just one description, then your friendships are probably okay for you. However, if one person is named several times, you should consider whether that's a friendship that's really right for you. And if two or more friends each match three or more descriptions, you might think about why you're surrounding yourself with people who are not positive influences in your life.

Here are some ideas for keeping friends who add to, rather than subtract from, the quality of your life:

- You can try to change a friend who's acting in ways that are mean, dangerous, or unhealthy. But your hands are tied if she's not ready and willing to modify her behavior. Then you might want to move away from that friendship before you get dragged down, too.
- Trust who you are and be yourself. If you can't be who you really are around your friends, do you still want those people taking up time in your life? Friends who are right for you won't make you pretend to be some-

thing you're not or make you feel uncomfortable when you're trying something new.

- Are you getting as much as you're giving in your friendships? (Remember that it's not just things but rather those important qualities like caring and kindness that count.) If the relationship is way off-kilter, then someone will get hurt sooner or later. Rebalance that equation to make it work, or encourage the relationship to die a natural death.
- Just because a friendship worked at one time in your life doesn't mean that it's a friendship that's meant to last forever. True friendships take up a lot of time, and that's fine if they're worth holding onto. But if a friend who used to be nice is now nasty, maybe it's time to send her packing.

Harriet Says:

My very best friend in junior high was an on-again, off-again friend who eventually drifted out of my life. We loved the same music, were attracted to the same boys, and had lots of fun together. But sometimes she lied, so it was hard for me to trust her completely. She made cruel comments about my brother who was mentally retarded, remarks that he didn't understand but really hurt me. And I can remember her making fun of me for not knowing some slang expressions. When I look at the quiz in this section, I realize that I had probably ignored some significant warning signs.

Are You Too Involved in Your Friends' Lives?

Caring about your friends is one thing; getting overly involved in their minute-to-minute lives is something else. Are you able to strike the right balance?

1. *One of your closest friends is planning a birthday party. You:*
   ___ a. will decide whether you're going when you actually receive the invitation.
   ___ b. ask her what kind of help she'll need.
   ___ c. give her the list of guests, decide on the menu, and think up a theme.

2. *A good friend just had a fight with her boyfriend. You:*
   ___ a. figure the best course of action is acting as if you don't know anything about what's going on—this is definitely not the kind of situation you want to get involved in.
   ___ b. act sympathetic and let her know that you're happy to listen to the whole story when she's ready to talk about the situation.
   ___ c. let her know that you didn't think they were right for each other anyway and that you can give her the names of at least five different boys who would be better for her.

3. *You and your friend are shopping at the mall. You:*
   ___ a. stay focused on what you need to buy and ignore what she's looking for.
   ___ b. ask for her opinion before you make your purchases and give her your ideas when she asks for them.

___ c. drag her to your favorite stores since you know what styles suit her best.

4. *A friend who's in your English class is having a hard time choosing a topic for her project. You:*
   ___ a. ignore her dilemma—you've got your own work to get done.
   ___ b. help her brainstorm some ideas, which should make her decision making a little easier.
   ___ c. tell her exactly what her topic should be—you just don't understand why it's taking her so long to make up her mind.

5. *Your friend's parents are going through a rough time—they might be getting divorced. You:*
   ___ a. figure this family problem is none of your business.
   ___ b. make sure she knows she can count on you as someone who will listen and not share what's been said—this is a very painful and personal matter for your friend.
   ___ c. tell her all about your other friends whose parents have divorced, and then you proceed to tell her how she should deal with her mom and dad now.

6. *One of your friends is not getting along with her math teacher. You:*
   ___ a. have enough trouble with your teachers—you're not going to offer any advice.
   ___ b. ask some questions that might help your friend figure out what she can do to repair the relationship.
   ___ c. march right up to the math teacher and demand that she stop treating your friend so unfairly.

7. *Two of your friends have been fighting a lot lately. Each one, independently, has been trying to draw you into the conflict. You:*
   ___ a. say, "No way."
   ___ b. tell them that you hate to see them fighting since they're both your friends and because of your relationship with each of them, you just can't take sides.
   ___ c. talk to each one privately, telling them exactly what they need to say to each other to clear up the misunderstanding. You are not going to tolerate conflict between two of your good friends.

8. *Your best friend's parents have decided she cannot go out on Friday nights any longer since she has trouble getting all her homework done on the weekend. You:*
   ___ a. can't imagine being grounded every Friday night. But at least it's not you this is happening to.
   ___ b. suggest that perhaps she can start her homework as soon as she comes home from school on Friday afternoon. Maybe her parents will reconsider if she begins to show greater initiative in getting the work done.
   ___ c. ask your parents to call your friend's parents. This is so unfair that something must be done.

Scoring

Mostly *A*s: Far, Faraway Friend. Are you sure you can call these people your friends? Sure, getting overly involved in your friends' lives is a problem, but putting so much distance between your life and theirs is telling them that you just don't care. Is that the message you're trying to convey? If it's not—maybe you just don't know how to help—start with these tips:

- Let your friends know that you are available for listening. Sometimes that's the best kind of help you can offer.
- Ask your friends whether they want more than an open heart and open ears. If they are interested in hearing your advice, give it generously, but don't force your friends to solve their problems your way.
- Help your friends solve problems by brainstorming with them. Before they jump into a solution that might not be best under the circumstances, suggest that they first list a bunch of different alternatives.

Mostly *B*s: Caring Companion. You have found the proper balance for dealing with your friends and their problems. You're not overly invested, but you're not distant, either. Your friends can count on you to listen and to suggest, but when you sense

Liz Says:

Usually, I don't give advice to my friends unless they ask for it. I don't want them to feel that I'm telling them how to live their lives and that I know more than they do. I have no problem giving advice on the Girl Scout Web site (www.girlscouts.org) that my mom and I write together. But that's because those girls are writing to us asking for our opinion. When my friends do ask for help, I tell them what I think they could do. But I don't make it seem as if any other way of solving the problem would be wrong.

that you need to back away, you quickly do so. You understand that sometimes your involvement is desirable, but at other times, it's best for you to keep a low profile. They know where to find you when the going gets rough.

Mostly *C*s: Bossy Bud. Your intentions are absolutely admirable. But the results are not always on target. You overwhelm your friends with your take-charge attitude. That's okay when they want your involvement, but you're not waiting around long enough to find out when they need you and when they don't. Take a step back. Remember that your friends' lives are separate from yours, no matter how much time you all spend together and no matter how you agree on most things. It's great that you care, but try showing a bit more restraint when it comes time for solving their problems.

Who, of all people, understands your feelings about boys? Sympathizes with you about your siblings? Giggles when you admit to embarrassing moments? Probably your closest friend. Although the friendships you have today may change—one best friend might leave town, while another might decide to move on to another crowd—they are and will continue to be a very big part of your life. Understanding what it takes to be a true friend is well worth the effort.

CHAPTER 7

He Likes Me, He Likes Me Not, He Likes Me . . .

Guys are probably taking up more of your thinking time these days, and maybe your telephone, online, and in-person time, too. Your parents may think you're too boy-crazy. Do you agree? What type makes your heart thump a little harder? Do your friends tell you that so-and-so likes you? How can you know for sure what he thinks? The quizzes in this chapter might give you just the hints you need.

Boys and You: How Do You Relate?

Do your thoughts freeze when that cute boy in your class walks by in the hall? And do your words get all jumbled up when you're trying to reply to a simple question he's asked? Or are you one of those girls who has always felt as comfortable with boys as you do with girls? Maybe you view guys more as friends than as potential romantic interests. Answer the questions in this quiz to see how you relate to the boys in your life.

1. *Your friend is having a party next week, and she told you that she's inviting boys and girls. You:*
   ___ a. have mixed feelings about going—on the one hand, you'd like to go to a co-ed party, but on the other hand, you think you'll be too self-conscious to relax and have a good time.
   ___ b. hope you like the kids who've been invited. It doesn't matter to you whether they're boys or girls—you just want to have fun.
   ___ c. better start thinking about what you're going to wear now—you want to be sure the guys notice you.

2. *The phone rings, and your dad yells out, "It's a boy!" You:*
   ___ a. cringe with embarrassment. How can you talk on the phone now that your dad has made such a fool of himself? You write a note to your dad: "Tell him that you don't know where I am" and then run out of the room so your dad really can't find you.
   ___ b. think, "Why is he making such a big deal about that?" It's not as if you don't have friends who happen to be boys.
   ___ c. can't wait to get to the phone to see who it is. Maybe it's that cute guy from your science class you've had a crush on for weeks.

3. *When your teacher assigns you to a project group in health class, you learn that you will be working with one other girl and two boys. You:*
   ___ a. wish that you didn't have to work with boys—you feel so ill at ease with them.
   ___ b. think that as long as they're all decent students and willing to contribute equally to the project, you're okay with the arrangement.

___ c. get all excited—here's your opportunity to spend an extended amount of time with boys!

4. *You've just learned that your neighbor's cousin, who's about your age, will be visiting from another state. He'll be staying with your neighbor during your winter school break. You:*
 ___ a. know it will be awkward trying to make conversation with him. You always get a little tongue-tied when it comes to talking to guys.
 ___ b. think it will be a great opportunity to find out about living in another state.
 ___ c. look forward to his visit—it should be fun to hang out with an interesting new guy during your vacation.

5. *Your math teacher likes to rotate the class seating arrangement from time to time. You've just been assigned to sit next to a boy who recently moved into your neighborhood. You:*
 ___ a. wish your teacher hadn't changed the way the tables were arranged—you felt comfortable with your old table mates.
 ___ b. welcome the opportunity to get to know a new classmate.
 ___ c. wonder whether sitting next to the new boy will make the class more exciting.

6. *Your friend's brother, who's a year older than you, seems to be paying more attention to you when you go over to her house. You:*
 ___ a. feel a little awkward with his new interest in you.
 ___ b. think this is a good chance to find out more about what classes will be like next year.
 ___ c. make sure you look your best now when you plan to stop over.

7. *In your gym class starting next week, the boys and girls will be playing volleyball together. You:*
   ___ a. wish it were all girls so you could feel more comfortable.
   ___ b. know you'll try your hardest no matter who's on your team.
   ___ c. hope certain boys you like will be on your team—here's your chance to impress them with how you play as well as how you look.

8. *When you and a group of your friends arrive at the lake one summer afternoon, you notice that a group of boys have already settled their stuff right at the water's edge. You:*
   ___ a. suggest that your friends find a place far from the boys—you don't really want them to watch your every move, particularly not while you're wearing your new bikini.
   ___ b. volunteer to introduce yourself and your friends to the group. It might be fun to meet some new kids.
   ___ c. are so glad you decided to wear your new bikini and hope that the boys will notice—and appreciate—what you're wearing.

9. *You and your best friend decide to get tickets to see the school musical. You:*
   ___ a. can enjoy the show since you know you won't have to make conversation with the adorable guys who are starring in it.
   ___ b. know a lot of guys and girls in the show, and it will be fun to see them perform.
   ___ c. will make sure to find a way to congratulate the star at the conclusion of the show—he's someone you've had your eye on for more than two months.

Scoring

Mostly *A*s: Not Ready Betty. You're aware that boys exist, but as soon as they get anywhere close to your personal sphere, you run for cover. Maybe you're a little shy around guys or just haven't had much experience with the opposite sex. That's okay—when you're ready to make a move, boys will still be around. Don't let your friends pressure you into doing something that you're not comfortable with. Remain true to your own needs and timetable.

Mostly *B*s: Comfy Kate. You're as much at ease with guys as with girls—they're all part of the same human race to you. That level of comfort will allow you to make and keep boys as friends, which means you'll be able to get a guy's perspective whenever you need it. Your feelings about certain boys might

Harriet Says:

Of course, I remember the boys I had crushes on in junior high. They were in a band, and I loved listening to them play. I don't think they knew I existed, so I had to be content worshipping them from afar and sending them anonymous letters from time to time. I was too shy and not enough of a risk taker to let them know my true feelings for them. My best friend and I spent a lot of time talking about boys, but I also focused on a lot of other interests at the time—schoolwork, girlfriends, music, books, and family.

change some time in the future, but you don't have to rush into romance because someone else might expect it of you.

Mostly *C*s: Fanatic Felicity. Guys are the center of the universe for you now. You'll do almost anything to get their attention. Whether you're in school, at the beach, or at home, your mind is on boys. It's normal to be more interested in guys now than when you were younger, but if you let your whole world revolve around them, you're missing out on lots of other opportunities for learning, friendship, and fun.

Does a Special Guy Like You?

What are the telltale signs that someone is interested in you as more than a friend? Are you reading the cues correctly, or are you allowing your hopes to distort reality? Think of a special guy and see how many of the descriptions match his behavior. That will give you a clue to his feelings for you.

1. *You have a big test coming up in science. He's one of the best students in the class and definitely doesn't need any help. But he asks you to study with him anyway.*
   ☑ Yes ❑ No

2. *He calls you on the telephone just to talk.*
   ☑ Yes ❑ No

3. *He shows up to watch you at a sports practice.*
   ☑ Yes ❑ No

4. *He has you on his online buddy list.*
   ❑ Yes ☑ No

5. *He IMs or calls you about a homework assignment even though he was in school that day.*
   ❑ Yes ❑ No
6. *He notices something that you're wearing and compliments you.*
   ❑ Yes ❑ No
7. *He asks if you'd like to work together on a school project.*
   ❑ Yes ❑ No
8. *You receive an unsigned Valentine's Day card, but you recognize his distinctive handwriting.*
   ❑ Yes ❑ No
9. *He joins you at your lunch table, even though you're sitting with all your girlfriends.*
   ❑ Yes ❑ No
10. *One day in class, you catch him looking in your direction instead of at the teacher.*
    ❑ Yes ❑ No
11. *He asks you to suggest a gift for his mom's birthday or sister's graduation.*
    ❑ Yes ❑ No
12. *He laughs louder than anyone else when you tell a joke, even one that's not very funny.*
    ❑ Yes ❑ No
13. *He walks home from the bus stop or school with you, even though he lives in a different direction.*
    ❑ Yes ❑ No
14. *He wants to know when your birthday is.*
    ❑ Yes ❑ No

15. *He gives you little gifts for no particular reason.*
 ❑ Yes ❑ No

16. *His friend tells you he likes you.*
 ❑ Yes ❑ No

Scoring

Give yourself one point for each "Yes" answer. The more points you have, the more he probably likes you.

0–3 points: Probably a Friend. He's not showing too many signs of interest. Either he really doesn't want to get involved in a relationship with you (maybe even with anyone), or he's the type who doesn't know how to show how he feels. If the latter is the case, it may be up to you to do a little more show and tell.

4–8 points: More Than a Friend. The signs are certainly pointing in the "in like" direction. If you're interested in him, you could respond to the signals that he's putting out there for the world to see. Then see what happens.

Liz Says:

I think this is a pretty good way to measure how much a guy likes you. You might want to add some of your own descriptions, ones you think might be signs that a particular boy is interested in you. Add those yes answers to your score, and then see how that guy probably feels about you.

9–16 points: Boyfriend. What are you waiting for? A marriage proposal? (Just kidding!) He's obviously very interested in being your boyfriend. Is that what you want? With all the positive messages he's sending your way, you know that the ball's in your court. The question is: Do you want to play?

Are You Ready for a Real Relationship?

It's one thing to talk to boys who are in your classes or hang out with a group of friends—both boys and girls. It's another to have an actual relationship, one in which you make plans together, see each other often, and care about each other. Are you ready for a real romance? Answer "True" or "False" to each of the statements in this quiz.

1. *I don't think I should start dating until I'm older.*
   ☒ True ☐ False
2. *I think about one particular boy a lot of the time.*
   ☐ True ☒ False
3. *I realize that I'm finding all kinds of reasons to talk to one special guy.*
   ☐ True ☒ False
4. *When I go online, I immediately check to see if he's online, too.*
   ☐ True ☒ False
5. *I think I'm better off going out with a group of friends than with one guy.*
   ☒ True ☐ False

6. *I try to look my best whenever I think I might run into this particular guy.*
   - ❑ True
   - ❑ False

7. *The big school dance is not going to be held for two months, but I'm already daydreaming about dancing with this guy.*
   - ❑ True
   - ❑ False

8. *I've told at least one member of my family about him.*
   - ❑ True
   - ❑ False

9. *He talks to me as though he's more of a boyfriend than a bud, but I wish he wouldn't.*
   - ❑ True
   - ❑ False

10. *He gave me a little gift for no reason at all, and it made my day.*
    - ❑ True
    - ❑ False

11. *I think of the boy I'm closest to more like a brother than a boyfriend.*
    - ❑ True
    - ❑ False

12. *When I see my friends with their boyfriends, I'm envious. I'm ready for a real relationship, too.*
    - ❑ True
    - ❑ False

13. *I'm looking for excuses to spend time with this special guy.*
    - ❑ True
    - ❑ False

14. *When he gives me a compliment, that counts more than if the exact same words came from anyone else.*
    - ❑ True
    - ❑ False

Scoring

Give yourself one point for answering true to statements 2, 3, 4, 6, 7, 8, 10, 12, 13, and 14 and for answering false to statements 1, 5, 9, and 11.

0–4 points: Friend. It's not that you don't like boys. But your interest is more platonic—you're looking at them as friend material, not as potential boyfriends. If and when you're ready for a real relationship, your heart and mind will let you know.

5–9 points: More Than a Friend. Your feelings are still a little mixed, but the relationship signals are getting stronger. The truth is, if one special guy shows you the right amount of interest, the scales might tip and push you into the next category. But

Harriet Says:

I was ready for a real relationship long before I had one. You have to remember that you might be ready before the right person is, or vice versa. I had friends who were dating at twelve and others who didn't start until college. Now, as a mother, I hope my children will not get hurt in their relationships. But I do recognize that they're the ones who will be navigating the waters. My role should be to stand by and offer support. Of course, I have been known to give unsolicited advice occasionally, and I might be tempted to do so again in the future.

don't rush into a relationship if you're not sure it's appropriate for you. And don't forget, if your parents will not allow you to date until you're older, that may keep you in the Friend category just a little longer.

10–14 points: Girlfriend. You're ready to roll into a relationship, and you know it. That doesn't mean that you're sworn for life to the particular guy you have a crush on now. But you can see yourself as part of a twosome. If, at any point, the relationship doesn't feel comfortable, remember that you're free to leave. But, unless the guy has really been awful to you, do it in a way that's honest but gentle. And if the guy has been a pig? He doesn't deserve any special consideration when you dump him.

What Makes You Fall Head over Heels?

Do you know why you develop a crush on one guy and not another? Answer these questions and you'll soon have a clue.

1. *Which of the following looks do you most like on a guy?*
   ___ a. khakis and sweater.
   ___ b. baggy pants, an earring, and shades.
   ___ c. T-shirt and jeans that show off a fit body.

2. *You're most interested in a guy who:*
   ___ a. is a solid student.
   ___ b. is a bit of a mystery.
   ___ c. is an athlete.

3. *A boy in your class asks if you'd like to get together on Friday night with some of his friends (you get to bring some of your friends along, too). You would be most interested in:*
   ___ a. going to a school dance.

___ b. doing something that doesn't require any advance planning—you like surprises.

___ c. going ice skating or playing tennis, any activity that gets you all moving.

4. *A guy you've had a crush on tells you something that makes your heart beat a little faster for him. What does he say?*

___ a. He's been named the student of the year.

___ b. He's going to be playing in the hot new band at school.

___ c. He's made it onto the varsity tennis team.

5. *Which compliment from a guy would make you like him more?*

___ a. He says that his mom likes your new hairstyle. Isn't it nice that he has the kind of relationship with his mom that they'd be talking about you—and your hair?

___ b. He tells you that your air of mystery is cool, which is interesting to you since that's what you find attractive about him.

___ c. He notices that your tennis skills have really improved since last season. Of course, he's quick to note that they weren't bad last year, but you're really a terrific player now.

6. *You walk into a party, and the boy you zoom in on:*

___ a. is helping the host serve the food and making polite conversation with everyone.

___ b. is someone you've never seen before.

___ c. looks like he arrived at the party straight from his soccer game.

7. *For your birthday, the guy you would fall head over heels for would get you:*

___ a. a simple piece of jewelry, maybe silver hoop earrings.

___ b. an exotic sculpture that he says matches your unique qualities.
___ c. a team T-shirt so you can wear matching outfits when you're out together.

8. *On Valentine's Day, you'd like him to surprise you with:*
___ a. one perfect rose.
___ b. a CD that he made especially for you—the songs range from rap to classic.
___ c. a framed poster of him that you can hang in your room and show off to all your friends.

9. *When the guy of your dreams meets your family for the first time:*
___ a. he shakes everyone's hands and talks in that polite, respectful tone of his.
___ b. no one knows quite what to make of him. He's definitely not like anyone else they've ever come across.
___ c. they all remark on how good-looking he is, and your brother or dad make an admiring comment about his muscular build.

10. *Your "head over heels" guy is known at school as someone:*
___ a. everyone likes and respects.
___ b. who keeps things interesting—you never know what he's going to say or do in class
___ c. who's good at every sport he tries.

Scoring

Mostly *A*s: You Like the "Clean-Cut Cutie" Type. You're likely to be bowled over by a guy who's a good student, dresses well in a preppy kind of way (but definitely doesn't go overboard with that kind of look), gets along with his family, and treats you well. He's a classic and classy kind of guy, a best-friend type. You're in for few surprises with him, buy you won't have to guess how he feels about you either.

Mostly *B*s: You Like the "Special Someone Who Surprises" Type. You like someone who can keep you guessing. He's definitely got an air of mystery about him, and he enjoys the fact that you like to keep the surprises coming, too. Maybe he's a musician; perhaps he's a writer. But whatever he does, he won't let his feelings totally hang out. The wild ride with him might get bumpy and zigzag all over the place, but you'll never complain about being bored.

Liz Says:

I like a mix of all of those types. I don't just look for one particular strong quality in a guy. I look for a little bit of everything. Now that I'm thinking about it, the guys I like do have some traits in common, but I still wouldn't consider them a specific type. I look for characteristics, such as a sense of humor, intelligence, and sensitivity. Of course, looks do come into play since usually you notice a guy's appearance before anything else. But then you get to know the inner guy—the things that make you like him even more, or make you not like him at all.

Mostly *C*s: You Like the "Hunk of Your Heart" Type. He's the one with the six-pack abs. He truly believes that his body is a temple, so he treats it well. Not that he's conceited about his attractive looks or his powerful athletic abilities—those qualities are just a part of who he's always been. Sports are an important part of his life, so he wants you out there running and playing, too. You could make beautiful music together on the field, the court, or the rink.

Are You Too Boy-Crazy?

Are you driving your friends and family crazy with your 24/7 focus on guys? Find out if you've gone totally overboard over boys by taking this quiz.

1. *When you're bored in one of your classes, you:*
   ___ a. start working on your homework.
   ___ b. doodle all over your notebooks boys' names and hearts.
   ___ c. think about your weekend plans—maybe a movie with a group of friends, both boys and girls.

2. *You're planning to redecorate your room. You:*
   ___ a. think the theme should be boys, boys, boys.
   ___ b. would like to hang some posters of guy music groups you like as well as movie posters.
   ___ c. decide to look at magazines for some fresh new ideas.

3. *When your science teacher asks you to choose a lab partner, you:*
   ___ a. think about who has qualities that would complement yours so you'll be a good working pair.

___ b. look around the room to see which cute guy might be fun to work with.

___ c. first think this might be a great opportunity to get to know one of the boys in your class better, but then you come to your senses and remind yourself that you're in school mainly to learn and that getting good grades is important.

4. *You're taking more and more time to get ready for school in the mornings. When your mom wants to know why, you realize that you:*

___ a. are spending most of your time daydreaming about a crush instead of focusing on getting out of the house on time.

___ b. are having a hard time getting out of bed—maybe you should try getting to sleep earlier at night.

___ c. spend a lot more time these days making sure that your hair and clothes look just right—you never know what boys might see you.

5. *When your friends casually ask you how you are, you:*

___ a. usually give them a quick update on anything new in your life.

___ b. ignore that question and instead give them a twenty-minute description of all the guys you have a crush on.

___ c. tell them how you really are and ask them the same question.

6. *Your best friend gave you one of those cartoon calendars with daily tear-off sheets. You:*

___ a. rewrite the captions and dialogue each day to reflect what's happening to you and the guys in your life.

___ b. like to look at the cartoons each day since they usually give you a chuckle.

___ c. hardly ever remember to tear off the sheets, so when it's April 10 in real life, you're probably still looking at February 19.

7. *When you have a sleepover with friends, the main topic of conversation is:*

___ a. your teachers and your other friends.

___ b. boys, boys, boys.

___ c. school and boys.

8. *Your brother, sister, or other family member has been known to tease you about your obsession with:*

___ a. boys, boys, boys.

___ b. a hot music group.

___ c. the collections that are taking over your room.

9. *When you've made plans to go some place with your friends, you would:*

___ a. only change those plans in an emergency—maybe your parents forced you to stay home to spend time with some relatives you've never met.

___ b. try to convince them that it would be more fun if you added a couple of boys to the group, but if your friends weren't interested, you wouldn't pursue the point.

___ c. insist that it would be much more fun if you could invite a few cute guys to join you, and if you couldn't persuade your friends, you probably would decide not to go with them.

10. *The latest copy of your favorite magazine arrives in the mail. You look through the table of contents and quickly turn to the article that's titled:*
    ___ a. "Boost Your Brainpower in Less Than a Month"
    ___ b. "Should You Change Your Style?"
    ___ c. "Catch the Crush You've Had Your Eye On"

Scoring

1. a: 1; b: 3; c: 2
2. a: 3; b: 2; c: 1

Harriet Says:

I remember distinctly the boy I had a crush on in fourth grade; I can even tell you his middle name (David), although it's been a long time since I was in fourth grade. I can also recall the full name of the boy I liked in fifth and sixth grades—the very same one for two whole years. Gary's slicked-back blond hair remains a vivid memory for me. I have no idea what happened to either of these boys. But they sure made my daydreaming more interesting back then. Although I spent a fair amount of time thinking about those boys (I don't remember actually saying more than a couple of words to either one of them), I was more of the "Semi-Serious About Guys" type. So I left plenty of room for my other interests (like my friends and music) and for school and my family.

3. a: 1; b: 3; c: 2
4. a: 3. b: 1; c: 2
5. a: 1; b: 3; c: 1
6. a: 3; b: 1; c: 1
7. a: 1; b: 3; c: 2
8. a: 3; b: 1; c: 1
9. a: 1; b: 2; c: 3
10. a: 1; b: 1; c: 3

10–16 points: Not Interested. Most likely, you have a wide variety of interests, which is healthy at your age. You have plenty of time to get serious about boys. If and when guys start taking up more of your energy, make sure you continue to keep some of your attention on who you really are and what you want out of life.

17–23 points: Semi-Serious About Guys. You're not boy-crazy, but your attention is definitely wandering a bit in that direction. Daydreaming about guys, developing crushes, and talking to your girlfriends about boys you like are typical at this stage of your life. Just make sure you continue to keep enough room in your heart and mind for other people and topics. You'll stay a lot more interesting that way.

24–30 points: One-Track Mind. Get a grip, girl! Yeah, boys are fun to think and talk about, but you're functioning as if nothing and no one else even exist. If the other people in your life are not already bored to tears by how totally boy-crazy you've become, their patience and tolerance will probably wear thin soon enough. It's fine—and normal—to be interested in guys. But you may be in danger of losing your focus on other things that count, too. Have you forgotten about school? Hobbies? Friends? Your family?

Your relationships with guys will have their ups and downs in the years ahead. Maybe your emotions are already on a roller-coaster ride depending on whether a boy you like talks to you or acts as if you're invisible. You probably have lots of questions about the shifting nature of your relationship with guys. Talking with your friends can help, but it might be even better to talk to and get advice from someone who's already navigated the confusing, choppy, always-changing waters—maybe your mom, an older sister or cousin, or an aunt. Try to make decisions based on what's right for you and what you're ready for.

CHAPTER 8

School Days or School Daze?

You spend more hours in school than anywhere else, except for your home—and a large part of that time you're sleeping. Do you make good use of your school day and your after-school hours? Are you trying to coast through doing the bare minimum? Or have you figured out what your learning style is and how to take advantage of it? How would you honestly assess your teacher's view of you? By answering the quizzes in this chapter, you'll pick up some ideas to help you make the most out of your school days.

What's Your Learning Style?

You have a unique learning style. Maybe you prefer to listen to tapes, while your best friend needs to see the written word. Perhaps you need to get down and dirty—actually manipulating objects to figure out how something works. Someone else might want to follow step-by-step diagrams. Find out more about what puts you into high learning gear with this quiz.

1. *Your health education teacher asks your class to prepare an antismoking message in any medium. You choose to:*
   ___ a. create a colorful poster.
   ___ b. get together with other students to put on a skit.
   ___ c. compose a song jingle.
   ___ d. write a short story in which the main character gets seriously ill from smoking.
   ___ e. make a radio public service announcement.
   ___ f. carry out an experiment to show the toxic ingredients of cigarettes.

2. *The hobby that most appeals to you is:*
   ___ a. painting.
   ___ b. team sports, such as soccer or softball.
   ___ c. playing a musical instrument.
   ___ d. journal writing.
   ___ e. listening to books on tape.
   ___ f. examining living and nonliving things under a microscope.

3. *Your social studies teacher announces that she will be giving a test the following week. You:*
   ___ a. hope that she will allow you to draw pictures of historical events.
   ___ b. plan to study while working out on the exercise bicycle you have at home.
   ___ c. expect to make up songs, which will include the dates and names of events—that way you won't forget them.
   ___ d. will carefully read the text and create notes to study from.
   ___ e. know that you'll do your best if you can study with a parent asking you questions.

___ f. will prepare by constructing a three-dimensional model of the countries you have been studying.

4. *The subject you do best in is:*
   ___ a. art.
   ___ b. gym.
   ___ c. music.
   ___ d. English.
   ___ e. social studies.
   ___ f. science.

5. *The activity that would help you learn the most is:*
   ___ a. looking at pictures of events.
   ___ b. acting out a skit on the subject.
   ___ c. memorizing a song containing the relevant facts.
   ___ d. reading an interesting book about the topic.
   ___ e. listening to your teacher explain the facts.
   ___ f. experimenting to discover what really happens.

6. *How do you think that most adults who know you well would describe your approach to learning?*
   ___ a. "She likes to get her information by looking at pictures and diagrams."
   ___ b. "She is almost always on the move."
   ___ c. "She is very musical."
   ___ d. "She needs to see the words on paper—she won't just take your word for it."
   ___ e. "She does best when she can listen to someone who's an expert on a topic."
   ___ f. "She is not the type to believe something is fact because someone stated it as such—she has to try things out herself."

Scoring

Look at your pattern of responses to see which learning style is your key to school success.

Mostly *A*s: Visual Learner. You do best when you can gather information by looking at pictures and diagrams, and when you can express yourself through art and design. The next time a teacher allows you to choose how you'd like to do a project, you might want to make a poster or design a Web site.

Liz Says:

I took this quiz myself and found out that I am mostly a "Visual Learner." I guess I always knew that I learned in this way, but through this quiz, I found out that I also learn through listening and reading. The one question that I knew exactly how to answer was 5. I chose "Reading an interesting book about the topic" as the activity that would most help me learn. In sixth grade I read a fascinating book about Eleanor of Aquitaine, and I still remember everything about her and her family. So reading works for me only if the book is really interesting since that was the only D answer I gave. I had a couple of "All Ears" responses, too, so I guess when the person who's explaining—a parent, a friend, or a teacher—does so in a clear way, that would be helpful to me. But if the person who's talking is dull, I wouldn't learn at all.

Mostly *B*s: Moving Target. You're not the type to take your learning lying down. The more you move, the better you like it. Sitting in class passively listening to a teacher drone on and on is pure torture for you. Instead of studying with a friend while you're both sitting together in the library, try taking a jog around the block with her—while discussing the topic you'll be tested on, of course.

Mostly *C*s: Music Maker. Your brain whirls into action to the sound of music. Use song lyrics to memorize names and events. Sing a song about a science formula you need to learn. Or just listen to music—as long as it's not too distracting—while you're studying.

Mostly *D*s: Reader Believer. You don't want others to tell you how it works; you want to see the facts in black and white. You recognize the magic of words—the ones you use to express your thoughts and feelings and the ones authors use to tell their stories or make their points. Reading opens up worlds of opportunities for you.

Mostly *E*s: All Ears. For you, hearing is believing. You probably get more out of what your teacher says than what she or he has written on the blackboard. If you don't understand something, you might be better off asking questions and listening carefully to the answers than working your way through a dense textbook.

Mostly *F*s: Living Lab. Why should you take someone's word for it when you can test it out yourself? That's your philosophy of learning. You need to experiment, to tear things apart to find answers. And you'll remember what you've learned better when you've done the work yourself.

What Club Should You Join?

Most schools offer a variety of extracurricular activities, ranging from sports teams to literary magazines to computer clubs. With all the choices, how do you decide which one to join? This quiz will help you decide.

1. *If you had to choose one of these activities to do in your free time, which one would it be?*
   ___ a. Creative writing
   ___ b. Playing a video or computer game
   ___ c. Putting on a play or show with friends
   ___ d. Playing sports
   ___ e. Doing an arts and crafts project
   ___ f. Making money
   ___ g. Playing a musical instrument
   ___ h. Investigating and solving problems
   ___ i. Learning a new language

2. *Although you have lots of time to make up your mind about a career, which one of those listed here interests you most right now?*
   ___ a. Writer or editor
   ___ b. Engineer
   ___ c. Performer
   ___ d. Professional athlete
   ___ e. Designer or artist
   ___ f. Business owner
   ___ g. Musician or band member
   ___ h. Lawyer
   ___ i. Travel guide

3. *Which of these reasons is most important in deciding which club to join?*
   ___ a. To explore a topic or activity that is new to you
   ___ b. To strengthen your skills in a subject or activity you already know
   ___ c. To meet new people
   ___ d. To do something together with your friends
   ___ e. To relax and have fun

4. *How much time do you have for an after-school activity?*
   ___ a. An hour or more a day throughout most of the year
   ___ b. An hour a week
   ___ c. A lot of time when it's off-season for your sport, but little or no time once the season starts
   ___ d. A couple of hours a week
   ___ e. It depends on what's happening with your homework and tests

Scoring

Matching your answers to questions 1 and 2 to the list below might suggest an interest in one or more clubs or organizations at school or in your community.

a: Literary magazine, school newspaper, yearbook, or book clubs

b: Computer, games, Web design, audiovisual, or chess clubs

c: Drama or theater club, school plays

d: Basketball, field or ice hockey, softball or baseball, soccer, swimming, cheerleading, lacrosse, tennis, volleyball, or track and field. Some schools also have fully equipped weight rooms available during school hours.

e: School plays—creating scenery and props; yearbook or literary magazine—taking photographs, drawing, or designing layout

f: Entrepreneur, business, math, or investment clubs

g: Band or orchestra

h: Student council, mock trials (students play the various roles from judge to jury), or peer mediation groups (students are trained to settle conflicts among their peers)

i: Language clubs (Spanish, French, Italian, Chinese, Japanese, etc.)

Matching your answer to question 3 to the list below will also help you decide which club to join.

a: You are interested in a club that would allow you to explore outside your usual experiences. For instance, if you're generally the quiet type but think it's time for a change, you might investigate something like trying to get elected to the student council or becoming a peer mediator.

b: You are interested in building on a strength you already have. Maybe you've been playing chess since you were six, and now you want more competition so you'll be able to increase your skills. If the chess club at school is involved in high-level tournaments, you might want to join.

c: You're less interested in the nature of the club than in making new friends. Go to a meeting of a club you typically wouldn't have joined, and see if the kids who are there are the type you'd like to get to know better. If they're not, try another club.

d: If you're too busy to spend much time with your friends, participating in a club with them would be the perfect opportunity for some together time. Decide with your friends which club that should be, and then join.

e: If you lead a very pressured life, the last thing you need is another activity that adds to your stress. Join a club that has a laid-back attitude, one in which you don't have to do anything more than show up and have fun.

The answer to question 4 is important to consider before signing up for a club. If a particular club requires several hours a week of your time and you're already beyond your limit in commitments, look elsewhere. Be realistic about the amount of time you can spare for an after-school activity.

If your school does not already have a club in an area you're interested in, you can try to start one. How? Take these steps:

- Put up flyers around school to let others know you're thinking about starting this club. Include information about how to contact you. If no one but you is interested in this club, you might as well drop the idea before

Harriet Says:

The only club activity I was involved in when I was a teen was a musical performance called "Sing." I think I would have enjoyed my years in junior high and high school more if I had gotten more involved in clubs. My friends were not joiners, and I was afraid to participate on my own. I wish I had—I could have developed some new skills and made new friends.

you've invested a lot of time in it. But, if you really, really want to establish this club, start a campaign to promote the possibilities among your classmates.

- Find a teacher or school administrator who can help you with the logistics of setting up a new school club.
- At your first meeting, decide on the club's goals as well as on the meeting time and day.

Finally, some clubs or groups will allow you to combine several of your interests so you won't have to choose among those you find appealing. For example, the Girl Scouts provides opportunities to lead, travel, play sports, take action in your community, strengthen business skills, spend time with friends, and meet new people.

Do You Study Smart?

Are you the kind of student who doesn't have to do much to ace a test or get rave reviews on projects? Or are you someone who needs to study really hard to get high or even decent grades? Take this quiz to find out not only where you stand but what you can do differently to improve the way you study.

1. *You find out on Monday that you have a major test on Friday. You:*
   ___ a. wait until Thursday night to begin to study.
   ___ b. begin to read your textbook on Wednesday.
   ___ c. make a schedule on Monday so that you can do a little bit of studying each day.

2. *The place where you study is:*
   ___ a. quiet, comfortable, and well lit.
   ___ b. in the kitchen where other family members often gather.
   ___ c. right in front of the television set so you won't miss your favorite show.

3. *When your teacher gives you an assignment, you:*
   ___ a. only sometimes remember to bring home the textbooks you need.
   ___ b. usually remember to bring home the textbooks you need.
   ___ c. always remember to bring home the textbooks you need.

4. *Before you begin to study for your English test, you:*
   ___ a. call another student from your class to find out whether the test really is the next day, since you evidently didn't write down the date in your agenda book.
   ___ b. make sure you have all your supplies right at hand—dictionary, pens, and paper, for example.
   ___ c. complain for at least fifteen minutes first.

5. *When you make a study date with friends, you:*
   ___ a. spend half of the time talking about topics not related to school and the other half preparing and eating a snack.
   ___ b. spend about half of the time gossiping and giggling and the rest of the time trying to study.
   ___ c. ask each other questions that will allow all of you to review the material.

6. *When you don't understand a topic in school, you:*
   ___ a. ask your friends who probably don't know any more than you do.
   ___ b. don't give it much thought—nobody knows everything, anyway.
   ___ c. stay after school for extra help from your teacher.

7. *One of the girls in your class tells you that she takes notes on the important information in each chapter of her textbook. You:*
   ___ a. know that you would never waste time doing that, and you can't imagine why she would.
   ___ b. think that this is a great idea, and you plan to give it a try, too.
   ___ c. are going to ask her to share her notes—you might as well take advantage of the hard work she's already done.

8. *Your science teacher tells your class that to be sufficiently prepared for the upcoming test, everyone needs to put in about two hours of study time. You decide:*
   ___ a. that it's best to break up your studying into half-hour periods. From past experience, you know that you'll learn more effectively if you take breaks.
   ___ b. to get the studying over with as soon as possible. You plan to study as soon as you come home from school—straight through from three to five in the afternoon.
   ___ c. to recalculate how much time you'll really need to study. You think you can get by with less than an hour.

Scoring

1. a: 1, b: 2, c: 3
2. a: 3, b: 2, c: 1

3. a: 1, b: 2, c: 3
4. a: 2, b: 3, c: 1
5. a: 1, b: 2, c: 3
6. a: 2, b: 1, c: 3
7. a: 1, b: 3, c: 2
8. a: 3, b: 2, c: 1

8–13 points: Clueless. When others were developing smart study habits, you were nowhere around. But, it's not too late. You have plenty of school years ahead. Start establishing new ways of work now by following the tips taken directly from the answers that are three-pointers on this quiz:

- As soon as you know you have an assignment or test coming up, make a schedule so you don't have to cram all your studying into a very tight time frame.
- Find a comfortable, well-lit space where you can minimize distractions for your regular study space. Keep needed supplies at hand so you can focus on your work without having to jump up every few minutes to find a ruler or a dictionary.
- Look at your assignments before you leave school, so you'll remember to bring home the books and supplies you need.
- When you plan to study with friends, settle down to work as quickly as possible. It's easy to get sidetracked and spend most of your time fooling around instead of studying.
- Take advantage of extra-help opportunities—for example, after-school help from teachers or a parent who can quiz you.
- Take notes on what you've read—the writing will embed the information in your head, and you'll only have to review the important pieces of information later on.

Liz Says:

Right now, I'm working on a project called "Homework's Effect on Your Life" with my friend Danielle. We've gotten together twice and worked very hard, but it hasn't seemed like a lot of work since we also had fun together and the topic is very interesting to both of us. We're trying to prove that students in our school get too much homework and that the heavy load interferes with sleep and our social life and generally increases stress. Our solution, which is part of the project, consists of the following points:

- School would start at 10 A.M. and end at 4 P.M.
- Teachers would give homework sheets at the beginning of each week with all assignments due on Friday.
- The homework limit for each subject would be one hour a week.
- No homework would be given on Fridays to allow students time to relax on the weekends with their friends and family.

I think most students will agree with our proposal, but I'm not sure our teachers will react well.

- Break up your study time into short periods, maybe a half-hour or so. Taking a breather from time to time can give you just the energy you need to keep you in peak studying form. But be sure you don't let those breaks stretch out too long.

14–18 points: So-So Student. You may not be clueless, but your study habits can still use a boost. Paying attention to the tips just mentioned can't hurt.

19–24 points: Smarty Pants. You obviously have a handle on smart ways to study. As your workload in school increases, keep those smart study skills in mind—you'll need them!

Are You a Teacher's Dream or Worst Nightmare?

All students can tell you who their favorite and most horrible teachers are. But teachers, too, have their dream students and the ones they'd like to send to someone else's classroom. If they were choosing, would teachers want to have you in their classes, or would you be the last one picked? Decide whether the statements in this quiz describe you or not.

1. *When your teacher asks a question and you know the answer, you wave your arm furiously in front of her, yelling, "I know, I know!"*
   ❑ True ❑ False

2. *Your teacher starts his class right on time every day. You walk into class late at least half of the time.*
   ❑ True ❑ False

3. *When you don't understand something your teacher has just said, you ask her to explain it and give an example.*
   ❑ True ❑ False

4. *Your best friend sits next to you in class, and you pass notes back and forth and whisper to her when you remember something important you have to share.*

   ☐ True ☒ False

5. *On those rare occasions when you forget to bring your homework to school, you don't blame the dog or your baby sister. You honestly admit that you forgot your homework.*

   ☒ True ☐ False

6. *You put a lot of effort into studying for tests so you'll do the best you can.*

   ☒ True ☐ False

7. *Your notebooks are well organized and neat, whether or not your teacher says he's going to be checking them.*

   ☒ True ☐ False

8. *You pay attention to your teacher, but when other students are talking, you don't bother to listen since they don't usually know any more than you do.*

   ☐ True ☒ False

9. *If your teacher is discussing something that's not particularly interesting to you, you noisily juggle your pens, tap on your desk, blow bubbles with your gum, or build a structure with erasers and paper clips.*

   ☐ True ☒ False

10. *When your teacher calls on you in class, you usually don't know the answer because you're working on homework for another class and not paying attention to what's going on in this class.*

    ☐ True ☒ False

11. *You interrupt your teacher with comments and questions that have nothing to do with the subject being discussed.*
❑ True ❑ False

12. *As soon as you get into class, you take out the books you need and copy down the homework written on the board.*
❑ True ❑ False

13. *When you finish your work before the rest of the class, you read quietly at your desk so you won't bother the other students.*
❑ True ❑ False

14. *You pack up your books ten minutes before the class actually ends so you'll be the first one out the door.*
❑ True ❑ False

15. *You interrupt your teacher while she's mid-sentence to tell her that it's time for the class to end.*
❑ True ❑ False

16. *You often come into class without the supplies you need, and just as the teacher is about to begin the lesson, you ask to borrow a pen or pencil.*
❑ True ❑ False

17. *You can't seem to keep your papers in order, and you have to ask for another copy at least half of the time.*
❑ True ❑ False

18. *You show enthusiasm about the subject under discussion, but you don't overdo it.*
❑ True ❑ False

19. *You take the initiative to work on extra-credit projects.*
❑ True ❑ False

20. *You participate in class on a regular basis by adding important information to the discussion, not just speaking to hear the sound of your own voice.*
❑ True ❑ False

Scoring

Give yourself one point for each of the following true statements: 3, 5, 6, 7, 12, 13, 18, 19, and 20. Give yourself one point for each of the following false statements: 1, 2, 4, 8, 9, 10, 11, 14, 15, 16, and 17.

0–5 points: Teacher's Nightmare. Being a Teacher's Nightmare can turn into an awful dream for you. If you keep annoying your teacher, you're making school life miserable not only for her or him but for you as well. Look at the statements where you didn't receive any credit, and you'll quickly learn what you can change. What qualities do teachers want to see in their stu-

Harriet Says:

Nightmare students are not just a problem for teachers; most students don't particularly appreciate the presence of disruptive, annoying classmates, either. While I didn't participate in class discussions the way my teachers would have liked—being shy prevented me from doing that—at least I didn't prevent others from learning.

Liz Says:

I don't interrupt my teachers and I'm usually prepared, but sometimes I don't pay attention in class when I find the subject boring. Lots of kids in my classes are nightmares to teachers—that's why it was so easy to make up this quiz. For example, one student keeps popping up out of his seat, and when he doesn't know the answer, he makes one up just to get the class laughing. Then there are the kids who have paper fights while the teacher is trying to explain a serious topic. Even good students can be a pain to teachers sometimes. Two of my friends once cracked up uncontrollably in the middle of their Spanish class when the teacher said something that was an inside joke for them. I'm sure she didn't appreciate the loud interruption.

dents? Enthusiasm, cooperation, intellectual curiosity, good time management, sincere effort, and respect for the teacher's position and the needs of other students. Choose at least one of these areas to work on—and get started right away.

6–10 points: "Needs Improvement" Student. You don't aggravate teachers enough to be their worst nightmare, but you'll have to work hard to find yourself in the "Ideal Student" category. Look at the preceding category to see the kinds of qualities teachers generally appreciate, and decide on an area where you can try a little harder. Then put a plan into action.

11–15 points: Good Student. You know what it takes to succeed in school. You're generally ready to learn, supplies and positive attitude in hand. Look at the questions where you didn't score points, and see if there are some minor changes you can make to further improve your relationship with your teachers.

16–20 points: Ideal Student. You're a teacher's dream—you're enthusiastic, cooperative, and motivated, just what a teacher wants in a student. Just make sure you don't get overly obsessive about pleasing your teachers. You still need to be true to your own needs and interests related to learning.

Are You Challenging Your Mind?

School's not the only place where you can learn. Museums, theaters, and zoos, for example, are also settings that encourage discovery. And travel to near and distant places can provide opportunities to explore the new and different. What about reading books (the ones that are not required—like this one?) and magazines or listening to CDs and tapes? Can't you stretch your mind with those resources? Take this quiz to see whether you're letting your mind slide or giving it a challenging workout.

1. *Each year, when it comes to reading books not required by a teacher, you:*
   ___ a. definitely read no more than three or four.
   ___ b. read up to one a month.
   ___ c. read more than a dozen.

2. *How many different kinds of music do you listen to—of your own free will?*
   ___ a. A couple

___ b. Three or four
___ c. At least five

3. *When your teacher gives the class an extra-credit assignment, you:*
   ___ a. do it to get the credit and to take advantage of a learning opportunity.
   ___ b. do it for the credit.
   ___ c. don't even bother thinking about doing it.

4. *Your school offers a variety of after-school activities. You:*
   ___ a. sign up for a couple with interesting titles—you might go if you have enough time.
   ___ b. sign up for whatever your friends will be in.
   ___ c. sign up for those that sound as if they will provide you with challenges you don't get during regular school hours.

5. *When your science teacher lets you choose how you will fulfill an assignment, you decide to:*
   ___ a. do it the easiest or fastest way.
   ___ b. do it in a way that will impress your teacher but is not particularly challenging.
   ___ c. find a way that allows you to learn something new.

6. *During your winter vacation from school, you:*
   ___ a. start a major project (perhaps creating a model rocket or writing a science fiction story) that is not related to school. You never have enough time to do those kinds of things while school is in session.
   ___ b. watch lots of television and basically veg out.
   ___ c. look ahead in your books, so you'll be ahead when school starts again.

7. *How do you usually keep up with current events?*
   ___ a. A few minutes of television or radio news once or twice a week
   ___ b. Regular reading of the newspaper
   ___ c. Who keeps up with the news?

8. *When you visit a new place on vacation, you like to:*
   ___ a. discover its history by exploring its landmarks and monuments.
   ___ b. find out what styles the stores are showing.
   ___ c. learn about its geography and natural environment.

Scoring

1. a: 1, b: 2, c: 3
2. a: 1, b: 2, c: 3
3. a: 3, b: 2, c: 1
4. a: 2, b: 1, c: 3
5. a: 1, b: 2, c: 3
6. a: 3, b: 1, c: 2
7. a: 2, b: 3, c: 1
8. a: 3, b: 1, c: 3

8–13 points: Shortchanger. You're taking the easy way out whenever you can, but you're not doing yourself a favor. Your mind becomes lazy, just as your body does, when you don't exercise it. Don't hide from opportunities that might challenge your brain. Instead, increase your storehouse of information and develop your thinking skills by tackling the more difficult path or seeking out answers in new ways.

14–18 points: Halfway There. You're doing some things right, but you could put greater effort into your learning life. The

Liz Says:

Sometimes I do things that challenge my mind without realizing it at the time. They just seem like fun. Listening to different kinds of music, creating story characters, and drawing pictures are all enjoyable ways for me to spend my free time. But my favorite challenging activity is playing a computer game called "The Sims," in which you create families and environments and solve their problems. Once in a while, my dad takes the CD for this game away because he thinks it's a total waste of time. It's true that I do play the game sometimes instead of doing school work, but playing "The Sims" can be creative. And I get to learn how to use money and time effectively. Maybe one day, I'll use my own time as wisely as I make my Sims characters use theirs.

more you use your brain, the better equipped you'll be to handle the challenges of school and jobs. Do crossword puzzles, read books, play word games, and figure out math problems in your head to push the learning envelope.

19–24 points: Challenger-in-Charge. Your attitude about learning gives you an edge in life. Your tendency to ask questions, to do more, to take advantage of new situations and people will pay off in the long run. Challenging yourself shouldn't be a burden—it can and should be fun!

You've been in school for a long time already, and you still have many years of schooling ahead. But if you learn how to study smart, recognize how you learn best, get on the good side of your teachers, and participate in enjoyable, enriching extracurricular activities, you'll make the most of your school experience and at the same time prepare yourself for a successful, happy future. What could be bad about that?

CHAPTER 9

What Did You Say?

Are you a good listener? How well do you get your messages across? What kind of impression do you make on others? Are you confident enough to stand up for yourself? Have you crossed the line from assertiveness to bullying? Conflicts between people often stem from miscommunication. She said one thing; you thought she meant the opposite. How you communicate is what the quizzes in this chapter are all about.

Do You Measure Up When It Comes to Communication?

Do you usually get your message across clearly? Or are you often misunderstood? See how well your communications skills measure up by taking this quiz.

1. *When you and your BFF are fighting, you:*
   ___ a. explain your perspective in a straightforward way.
   ___ b. scream louder than she can so you don't have to listen to her.

___ c. have a hard time listening to her side even though you know she might have a point.

2. *How often do your friends have to ask you to explain what you mean?*
   ___ a. Whenever you open your mouth
   ___ b. Sometimes
   ___ c. Once in a great while

3. *When you disagree with your parents about an important rule, like the time of your curfew, you:*
   ___ a. present one argument after another, barely pausing to taking a breath.
   ___ b. tell them how you feel and listen to their viewpoint.
   ___ c. demand to be heard.

4. *Because of your skills, you would most likely be asked to join the:*
   ___ a. debate team.
   ___ b. homework helpers committee.
   ___ c. community beautification club.

5. *Your philosophy about communication is:*
   ___ a. honesty is the best policy.
   ___ b. beating around the bush can avoid conflicts.
   ___ c. use humor to break the ice.

6. *When your friends don't seem to understand how you're feeling about an issue, you:*
   ___ a. just get angry. They've known you long enough to be able to read your mind.
   ___ b. explain clearly how you feel, never assuming that they should have the same emotions as you do.
   ___ c. give them a few clues so they can figure out what's going on in your emotional world.

7. *On your report card, you might receive a comment such as:*
   ___ a. "She should participate in class more often since she seems to have good ideas."
   ___ b. "She communicates her ideas clearly in class."
   ___ c. "If her communication skills don't improve, I may forget that she's even in my class."

8. *Which of the following sounds most like you?*
   ___ a. "I don't know, but I might possibly want to go somewhere."
   ___ b. "Maybe I could go with you—if you wanted me to, that is."
   ___ c. "I'd like to go to the party tonight."

Scoring

1. a: 3, b: 1, c: 2
2. a: 1, b: 2, c: 3
3. a: 2, b: 3, c: 1
4. a: 3, b: 2, c: 1
5. a: 3, b: 1, c: 2
6. a: 1, b: 3, c: 2
7. a: 2, b: 3, c: 1
8. a: 1, b: 1, c: 3

8–13 points: Misunderstood. You expect others to understand what you're thinking and feeling even though you're not expressing yourself clearly. Stop requiring your friends and family to be mind readers, and start communicating more clearly. Here are some tips:

- Say what you mean. Compare "I want to go to the party" to "I think I might possibly go to the party, but I

Harriet Says:

Many girls have gotten into the habit of using lots of modifying words—*maybe, well, you know, sort of, I think*—instead of getting right to the point. You don't have to beat yourself up for being misunderstood or for sounding weaker than you'd like. Instead, you can use the puzzled or uninterested facial expressions of those listening to you to help you communicate more effectively the next time. Since I was a college teacher for many years, I learned to read the faces of my students. I could easily distinguish boredom from lack of understanding. I would adapt my lesson to create more excitement if that was needed or use a concrete example to clarify a particularly difficult concept.

don't really know." If your message is supposed to convey that you do want to go to the party, the first sentence does the job far better than the second one.

- Ask someone to listen critically to the way you communicate, and then give you suggestions. Be sure to say you'd appreciate an honest appraisal since you want to improve your skills, not hear empty compliments.
- Practice your communication skills every chance you get—in school, in conversations with your family and friends, in club meetings.
- Remind yourself not to ramble on but rather to make one clear point, and then pause before making your next point.

14–18 points: Good Communicator. You have good communication skills, but you could use a bit more practice and guidance from others to get even better. Pay attention to classmates and friends who communicate well. What are they doing that you might try?

19–24 points: Ready for Prime Time. Either you're a natural, or you've worked hard to become an effective communicator. Whatever the case, keep using those skills so they'll be available when you need them, which will be often.

How Confident Do You Appear?

You walk into a party. Do you look like you'd rather be anywhere else but there, or do you stride in with an unmistakable air of confidence? It's your turn to make a speech in class. Do you walk up to the front of the room with grace and ease, or do you timidly make your way up the aisle with your head down and hands visibly shaking? Answer these questions to discover how confident you appear to others.

1. *Your social studies teacher has just called on you to deliver your three-minute presentation on the Industrial Revolution. You:*

 ___ a. are excited that you've finally gotten called on. You have a great speech to give, and you're going to start off with a joke that you know will put the class into hysterics.

 ___ b. are well-prepared so you feel comfortable about what you're going to say, but you're a little nervous about facing all the other students.

 ___ c. can feel your heart pounding and your legs turning to pudding as you slowly rise from your seat. Your face turns beet red as you slowly make your way to the front of the room.

2. *You've been a member of the Literary Magazine club for months, and this afternoon everyone is supposed to read one of the pieces they've written to the rest of the group. You:*
   ___ a. hope you'll get called on first. You love reading aloud, particularly when it's something you've written, and you're proud of the piece you prepared.
   ___ b. would prefer not to read aloud, since you know that's not your strength. On the other hand, you think your piece is pretty good, and you should be able to dramatize it well enough for the others to get a feel for the mood you were trying for.
   ___ c. decide you're going to skip this meeting and give the piece to one of the other members to read for you. You enjoy the writing, but the thought of actually reading what you've written is more than you can handle.

3. *You have a once-in-a-lifetime opportunity—to appear on a television talk show. You:*
   ___ a. can't wait for your big moment of fame. You expect your confidence to shine right through the television screen—maybe you'll be asked to anchor your very own show after this appearance.
   ___ b. are excited about this opportunity but definitely nervous. You plan to practice ahead of time so when you're on the air, you'll look a little more confident than you feel.
   ___ c. know all your friends would die for this kind of opportunity, but you know you'd just die of embar-

rassment when you can't get a single word out of your mouth. You'll have to pass up this opportunity.

4. *Twenty percent of your grade in your Spanish class is based on your oral work. You:*
   ___ a. speak in a loud, clear voice when your teacher calls on you since you know your grade depends on it.
   ___ b. speak as confidently as you can when it's your turn, but your voice sometimes quivers a bit since you do get a little anxious.
   ___ c. feel almost paralyzed with fear when you hear your name, and you speak in an unnatural voice that even you hardly recognize as your own.

5. *When you enter a party at which you know very few people, you:*
   ___ a. say hi to the people you do know and then enthusiastically introduce yourself to a few people you don't know.
   ___ b. hang out with the people you know and glance around with interest at some of the people you haven't met—maybe one of them will start up a conversation.
   ___ c. make sure you surround yourself with the few people you know so no one new will even attempt to talk to you.

6. *When you and your friends are deciding what you want to do one Saturday afternoon, you:*
   ___ a. express your idea clearly and confidently and suggest that everyone take a vote.
   ___ b. tell them your idea when asked but go along with whatever your friends want to do.
   ___ c. don't say anything and do whatever your friends want.

7. *You're at your lunch table with your friends when a bunch of cute guys come over. You:*
   ___ a. start talking to one of them right away about something funny that happened in your English class that morning.
   ___ b. wait for one of them to say hi to you and then talk to him about the French test that's coming up that afternoon.
   ___ c. focus intently on your sandwich as you continue to eat. You don't say a word to anyone.

8. *You're at your friend's house for dinner. You:*
   ___ a. obviously enjoy the conversation and express your views, even when you're not asked.
   ___ b. make comments about different subjects from time to time and answer questions, but mainly you just listen.
   ___ c. eat and listen quietly, and you talk only when someone directly asks you a question.

Scoring

Mostly *A*s: Ms. Confidence U.S.A. You walk, talk, and breathe with confidence. Wherever you go, you make sure that the world notices you. Your strong presence will allow you to move ahead and take advantage of all kinds of opportunities. You won't ever allow yourself to be left out in the cold. The minus side is that you may sometimes ignore other people's ideas or feelings. As long as you keep that in mind, go girl, and enjoy life!

Mostly *B*s: Confidence Apprentice. You're somewhere in the middle of the confidence range. With just a little push, you speak up and stand up tall. You might try practicing stronger speech and body language so that when your teacher calls on you or you're at dinner with people you don't know well, you'll look more comfortable. In time, you'll probably find that even if you start out pretending to be self-assured (meanwhile you're shaking inside), you'll eventually learn to feel more confident. When your more confident manner on the outside gets a positive reaction from others, that internal confidence meter will register higher.

Harriet Says:

When I think back to my preteen and teen years, I can recall lots of instances in which I behaved just like a "Timid Mouse." It wasn't my lack of confidence in my abilities that held me back. I knew I was smart. But I was afraid that someone might laugh if I didn't pronounce a word right or think poorly of me if I couldn't answer the follow-up question to one I'd already answered. Or perhaps I thought someone would make fun of the way I dressed (my family had very little money then). Whatever the reasons, I did not appear very confident, particularly in school and around people I didn't know well. But I also knew that if I wanted to become a teacher, which was my career aspiration at that time, I would have to learn to become more confident. And, fortunately, that is something you can learn. I also realized that people who are more confident seemed to have more fun, and I certainly didn't want to be left out.

Mostly *C*s: Timid Mouse. You've got your work cut out for you, but try not to be discouraged. Lots of girls are timid at this stage of life. But if you're sufficiently motivated, you can make some big changes in the way you act. And you'll be pleasantly surprised that the more you act in a way that beams confidence to the world, the more confident you'll become—even if you start out playing a role. There are a few tips on the next page for you to try.

Liz Says:

Last week I took part in a press conference because of my role as an online advice columnist (the "Ask Dr. M" section of the Girl Scout Web site: www.girlscouts.org). When I was first asked to be a speaker at a conference unveiling a Girl Scout study about girls and the Internet, I wasn't sure I wanted to do it because I knew that I would be nervous. But then I decided it would be interesting and a good learning experience for me. And when I heard that some of my favorite magazines were going to send editors to the event, I decided this could almost be fun. Actually, when it came time to make my speech, I wasn't as nervous as I thought I would be. By the time the questions from the reporters came, I was feeling pretty comfortable about speaking. The technique I use to build my confidence is to pretend I'm already confident. I have found that each time I do some kind of public speaking, I get better at it, and, more important, it really does get easier.

- Talk to the mirror in a confident voice. If you have a tape recorder, tape your voice. Listen to how you sound. Try for that tone of voice in situations in which you're usually lacking in confidence.
- Use self-talk to build your confidence. Before walking into a situation where you could use a confidence boost, tell yourself that you're strong and powerful.
- Practice your confident walk around your house or along a shopping area where you can see your reflection in the glass windows.
- After you've been in a situation in which you did not think you acted with much confidence, analyze what you could have done or said differently. But don't dwell on the "should haves." Instead, decide how and when you will incorporate the alternate actions you identified.

Can You Stand Up for Yourself and Others?

You've probably already found yourself in lots of situations in which someone said something that was unfair to you or to a person you care about or in which you were asked to do something that you felt was wrong. How did you react? Answer these questions to find out whether you have what it takes to stand up for yourself and others.

1. *If a friend asks you to help her cheat on a test, you:*

   ___ a. say okay timidly and let her cheat off of your test.

   _✓_ b. confidently tell her that you don't feel comfortable helping her because you think that cheating is wrong.

___ c. yell at her for putting you in such an awkward situation and ask her, "Do you think I'm your slave or something?"

2. *When you hear one of your guy friends say that girls can't play sports, you:*

___ a. ignore it and act like you didn't hear him say it.

___ b. tell him that it isn't true and that his comment is very sexist.

___ c. confront him angrily, saying that he's a chauvinistic pig and that if he says anything like that again, you'll quit being his friend.

3. *A friend says that she just found out that the coffee shop that the two of you go to sometimes pays higher salaries to men than to women. You:*

___ a. agree with her that it's not fair, and then you go back to whatever you were doing.

___ b. decide to find out if that really is true and, if it is, figure out what actions you can take to convince the manager that the pay scale should be equal.

___ c. go straight to the manager, shouting that his practices are unfair and that if he doesn't change them immediately, you'll make sure that you and your friends never go there again.

4. *When you overhear one of your classmates say that African Americans can't play the flute well right in front of a girl who is African American and plays the flute, you:*

___ a. wish you could say something in response since you know that what she said is not true, but you keep quiet.

___ b. calmly explain to your classmate that she shouldn't have said that because it is an unfair generalization and that she probably should apologize to the African American girl who was standing nearby when the comment was made.

___ c. go right up to your classmate and scream at her at the top of your lungs that she's a disgusting racist.

5. *At a party someone asks you if you want a beer. You say:*

___ a. "I don't know. I mean, I guess not."

___ b. "No, thanks. I don't drink."

___ c. "No way! What do you think I am—an idiot? Anyone who drinks has got to be the stupidest person in the world."

6. *You're hanging out with some of your friends when they start to make fun of one of your best friends who's not around. You:*

___ a. ignore what they're saying even though listening makes you feel very disloyal.

___ b. tell your friends that what they're saying is making you uncomfortable and really isn't fair since your friend isn't there to defend herself.

___ c. blast your friends for their mean comments and threaten to tell your best friend what you've just heard.

7. *You have a learning disability, which allows you to have extra time on standardized tests. When someone tells you that you have an unfair advantage, you:*

___ a. mumble something quickly and then rush off feeling very hurt.

___ b. calmly explain that you have a learning disability and that you need that extra time because it takes you longer to process the test questions.

___ c. explode with "Are you saying that I'm stupid? *You're* the one who's stupid."

8. *You're talking with some friends in the school cafeteria, when one of them makes a foolish comment. Another friend then says, "You're gay." You:*
   ___ a. hope that someone will say that using the word *gay* in that way is wrong, but you're just too shy to say that.
   ___ b. speak up and say that the comment was homophobic even if he didn't mean it that way.
   ___ c. tell your friend exactly how you feel. And you don't leave out the part about him being a homophobic idiot.

Scoring

Mostly *A*s: Scaredy Cat. You're not doing yourself or the people you care about any favors with your passive reactions. Actually, keeping your real reactions inside is probably eating away at your self-esteem—it can't feel good to be afraid to stand up to others when you know you should. You're letting the people around you believe that you either don't care about their mean-spirited comments or agree with them. Either way you lose. What can you do? Here are some tips:

- Role-play some situations, maybe with a parent or a close friend, in which you try out responses that are more assertive than you're used to. Instead of listening quietly to a racist or sexist comment, calmly explain why those words are unfair. Eventually, you'll be able to be assertive for real.
- Tell yourself that you'll respect yourself more once you are able to stand up to others. Convince yourself, with a conversation in your head, that you are strong enough to speak up. Imagine how good you'll feel when you start acting in a more assertive way.
- Show yourself that you have the courage to be assertive. Start with a very small action, maybe by saying some-

thing mildly assertive to a cousin or sibling, someone who's not particularly threatening. Then you can work up to confronting more difficult situations and people.

Mostly *B*s: Confident Cookie. You keep your cool, even in tough situations. You don't let people get away with put-downs, but you handle them with grace and calm instead of wild anger. Upsetting other people is not the point of your assertiveness. Rather, teaching or setting the record straight is what you have in mind. Your assertive style will not always lead to enlightened attitudes or respect for your viewpoint, but in the end you'll always have your self-respect.

Mostly *C*s: Nuclear Reactor. You may be absolutely right to stand up to others, but when you explode with anger instead of

Harriet Says:

Back in junior high, I usually chose to ignore the slights others slung at me. In my head, I said all the right things, but the words never actually came out of my mouth. The other extreme, aggression, has never been my style, so that's never been an issue for me. As I got older, I began to force myself—no, it didn't come naturally to me—to speak up. Not only did it feel good, but the more I responded with confidence, the easier it became. And that was particularly true in those situations in which people have needed me to come to their defense because they couldn't speak up for themselves.

using calm logic, you probably lose your audience and any chance you have to change their minds. It may be difficult for you to control your aggression, but in the long run, people pay more attention to assertive responses, like the *B* ones in this quiz. And isn't that what you're after? How can you control your hostile reactions? Here are a couple of ideas:

- Think about how you would feel as the victim of someone else's aggressive behavior. The next time you're tempted to attack someone with harsh words, picture yourself in her shoes and act the way you'd want her to treat you.
- Practice some assertive, less hostile, ways to stand up for yourself. Remind yourself that quiet logic is often more powerful than noisy emotion. And count to ten before you explode.

Are You a Good Listener?

You're asked to listen all the time—when your parents tell you what to do, when your teacher explains a formula, when a friend confides in you about her problem. How well do you really listen to what they're saying? Find out by checking off how you'd react in each of the following situations.

1. *When your friend calls you on the telephone and tells you that she needs your advice about a problem she's having with her parents, check off each of the following that you're likely to do.*
   ___ a. Figure out what to tell her before she's half-finished with her story.
   ___ b. Allow your mind to wander to one or more other subjects while she's still telling her story.

___ c. Interrupt to tell her about a similar situation that happened to you.
___ d. Ask questions once in a while to make sure you understand the whole situation.
___ e. Turn off the television or radio so your friend can have your full attention.

2. *When your teacher is explaining a complicated subject, check off each of the following you're likely to do.*
___ a. Daydream about an entirely different topic.
___ b. Write a note to another classmate about a party that's taking place on the weekend.
___ c. Start working on your homework.
___ d. Ask questions if a part of the explanation is not clear.
___ e. Take notes to help you remember the main points.

3. *When your parents are discussing vacation plans during dinner, check off each of the following you're likely to do.*
___ a. Ask to be excused.
___ b. Bring up an unrelated subject.
___ c. Start humming the song that's playing in your head.
___ d. Show your agreement by nodding your head.
___ e. Listen quietly and respectfully until it's your turn to offer your opinion.

Scoring

Give yourself one point for each *A, B,* and *C* answer you've checked on items 1, 2, and 3. Subtract one point for each *D* or *E* answer you've checked on those items.

–6 to –2 points: Active Listener. Your friends, family, and other people in your life are fortunate that you know how to give them your full, undivided attention. By engaging in active listening, you're letting them know that you care about what they think and feel. And when you listen carefully in school, you're probably learning more than you would if you only listened in a half-hearted way.

–1 to +3: Semi-Active Listener. You evidently pay attention some of the time or in some situations. Try to keep in mind that communication is more likely to go smoothly when both people listen in an active way, caring about what's being said and tuning out potential distractions.

+4 to +9: Inattentive Listener. This time a high score is not a good thing. You're not paying attention well enough to really

Liz Says:

I am a pretty good listener. I listen to other people most of the time, but sometimes I just pretend to listen. In class if the teacher is talking about something that I already know, I'll act like I'm paying attention, but I'm not. Also, if I'm talking on the phone with one of my friends and she's just telling me something that isn't really important or just goes on too long, I sometimes do something else, but I'm still half-paying attention, just like in school. I don't want to be rude, so I don't change the subject or say something that shows that I'm not interested.

find out what other people are saying. Miscommunication could be the result. Most likely you'd like other people to pay attention to you when you speak. Show them the same consideration. Do the following:

- Stop whatever you were doing and listen quietly.
- Show that you're interested by leaning forward and making direct eye contact.
- Ask relevant questions and repeat back some of what you've heard to make sure the two of you are on the same wavelength.
- Nod your head to show agreement, but only when you mean it.

Are You a Bully?

Have you ever picked on others who are weaker, smaller, or quieter than you? Do you get a secret thrill out of teasing younger kids when you know no one is around to defend them? See whether you're a bully by answering "True" or "False" to these statements. If you find out that you are a bully, the good news is that you can change.

1. *When I'm angry, I often take it out on my younger siblings or on kids in school who are smaller than me.*

   ❏ True ❏ False

2. *I like the power I feel when I tease other kids.*

   ❏ True ❏ False

3. *When I lose a game, I often accuse the person I'm playing with of cheating.*

   ❏ True ❏ False

4. *When I don't like someone, I give her dirty looks whenever I can just to be sure she knows that I can't stand her.*
   ❑ True ❑ False

5. *I have spread rumors about ex-friends to get back at them.*
   ❑ True ❑ False

6. *I like to get my friends to laugh by making fun of other people.*
   ❑ True ❑ False

7. *When I'm annoyed with a friend, I totally ignore her. I want her to beg me for forgiveness.*
   ❑ True ❑ False

8. *When I have something to say, I tend to just interrupt whoever is speaking.*
   ❑ True ❑ False

9. *It makes me even angrier when people ignore me when I pick on them.*
   ❑ True ❑ False

10. *I'm jealous when my friends do better than me on a test, so if that happens, I try to sabotage their performance on the next test.*
    ❑ True ❑ False

11. *When someone says or does something mean to me, I get even by taking revenge that is even meaner than anything they've said or done, even resorting to physical violence if I have to.*
    ❑ True ❑ False

12. *When I hear classmates asking for help from the teacher, I let others know how stupid their questions are.*
    ❑ True ❑ False

Harriet Says:

One day when I was a sophomore in high school, a girl, who probably didn't have anything better to do, followed me up the stairs from the cafeteria trying to burn me with the end of her lit cigarette. I had never done anything to her, so my guess is that she picked on me because she decided I wasn't going to tell on her, and I didn't. But I certainly avoided her, and I watched my back every time I climbed the stairs. Although I never asked for help with the bully who bothered me, I would certainly recommend that you tell an adult if something like what happened to me occurs to you. Bullying, particularly physical violence, is taken more seriously these days, and it should never be tolerated at school.

Scoring

Count up the number of true statements.

0–3 points: Kind Kid. You're generally a decent, caring person. Maybe once in a while you do something that isn't so nice, but that's normal. Look at the statements, if any, that you marked as true, and try to become more aware of your tendency to act in a not-so-nice way in those situations.

4–6 points: Teaser Trainee. You seem to have started down the path of being hurtful to others—maybe to get attention for yourself, to exert your power, or to feel more in control of your life. Maybe you're treating others in a way that is similar to the way that you've been treated. But you can learn more positive ways to treat others. Start by reviewing the items that you said were true, and decide (maybe with some help from an adult or friend you trust) what you can do differently when you're angry, frustrated, or just want some attention.

7–12 points: Big Bully. If you see a lot of yourself in the statements in this quiz, you're a bully—plain and simple. And you need to do something about it now. If you don't want to go through life as a bully (and why would you want to be the kind of person everyone hates?), ask a parent, a guidance counselor, or another adult for help in changing a very destructive pattern of behavior.

Communicating effectively plays a part in your school life, your relationships with your friends and family, and later on your success at work. Get a head start by working now on those skills that will make a difference in every important area of your life. The quizzes in this chapter should have helped you recognize your strengths and weaknesses. What's left for you to do? Practice every chance you get to speak with confidence, listen well, stand up for yourself, and talk to others with respect.

CHAPTER 10

Growing Older, Getting Better

Do you make smart choices when you're faced with tough situations? Are you on a path that will lead you to success in school and later in a career? Have you had the opportunity to learn from a role model, and are you ready to be one yourself? This chapter is about preparing for your future. Find out what may be in store for you.

Can You Make Tough Decisions and Smart Choices?

This is a time in your life when you have to make difficult decisions. How often do you come up with the smartest choice? Find out by answering these questions.

1. *You've been invited to a party by a girl who's a couple of years older than you. You decide to go since you feel cool about hanging out with a group that's older than your usual crowd. When*

you get to the party, you see that no adults are around to supervise and that several of the guests are drinking beer and smoking. You:

✓ a. call your parents and ask them to pick you up right away. You know you shouldn't be at a party where people are smoking and drinking.

__ b. decline the offer of a cigarette or a drink, but you decide to stay so you can tell your friends about the cool time you had with this sophisticated group.

__ c. decide to try a beer, just to see what everyone's talking about.

2. *A friend has told you that she keeps her weight down by smoking. You:*

__ a. figure if it works for her, maybe you should try it, too, since the pounds have been creeping up on you the past couple of months.

✓ b. tell her that she'd be better off watching her diet and exercising more; that's what you do to keep your weight in a normal healthy range.

__ c. know that smoking is very bad for your health, so you're not going to try it. But maybe a crash diet could take off the extra weight that you've put on this winter.

3. *It's exam time at school, and you're feeling pretty stressed out. You:*

__ a. call a close friend to talk about how you feel. She's usually someone you can call on to help you out when you're not feeling so great.

✓ b. make a schedule that will allow you to space out your studying and still give you time for breaks.

__ c. scream at your family and pick on your friends. You know you shouldn't take out your stress on the people you care about, but you can't seem to help yourself.

4. *You just spent the last hour watching TV and eating loads of junk food. You:*

   ✓ a. decide that you're going to do a better job of staying away from both. You make a list of some other activities that would be relaxing and healthier, and you're definitely going to start doing some of them.

   ___ b. have heard that some girls force themselves to throw up when they've had too much to eat and think you should try it.

   ___ c. write in your journal about how disgusted you are with your behavior.

5. *When someone makes a nasty remark about you, you:*

   ___ a. immediately jump down her throat with an equally cutting remark of your own.

   ✓ b. keep your cool as you let her know that you don't appreciate her mean comment.

   ___ c. turn away quickly so she won't see the tears welling up in your eyes. You know you should say something, but you just can't.

6. *Your family has had money problems for a few months now, and you've been asked to cut down on your expenses. You:*

   ___ a. don't see why you should have to cut into your lifestyle just because your parents don't have a handle on managing money.

   ___ b. work out a personal budget that will help to ease your family's financial burden.

   ✓ c. offer to take on more baby-sitting, lawn work, or other odd jobs so you won't need an allowance any longer.

7. *Your school is holding auditions for a new play. You:*
   - ✓ a. ask your best friends if they're going to try out. If a couple of them are planning to audition, you'll probably do so, too.
   - ___ b. can't imagine why anyone would want to make a fool of herself in front of the whole school. You're certainly not going to try out for a part.
   - ___ c. think that being in a play might be a great way to meet new people and to learn to feel more comfortable speaking in front of others. You're definitely going to try out.

8. *You just read an article about girls who've met their boyfriends in public chat rooms online. You:*
   - ✓ a. are not going to try to meet anyone that way—it's just too dangerous.
   - ___ b. decide that it might be fun to see if you can start a romance that way, but you're definitely not telling your parents. You know that they would never understand.
   - ___ c. ask your friends what they've heard about this new way of meeting and dating.

SCORING

1. a: 3, b: 2, c: 1
2. a: 1, b: 3, c: 2
3. a: 2, b: 3, c: 1
4. a: 3, b: 1, c: 2
5. a: 1, b: 3, c: 2
6. a: 1, b: 3, c: 3
7. a: 2, b: 1, c: 3
8. a: 3, b: 1, c: 2

8–12 points: Risky Decision Maker. You have a tendency to make decisions without thinking through all the consequences. Or maybe you just ignore anything you don't want to hear. Why else would you think it's okay to try a beer to look cool or a cigarette to stay slim? Some of the choices you've made on this quiz may be downright dangerous—did you answer *B* to 4 or 8, for example? If you did, you may be headed for real trouble, and you should talk to a parent or a school counselor who can help you make better choices.

13–17 points: B– Decision Maker. You've got some of this decision-making stuff down pat, but you may have to bone up on a couple of areas. Look at the questions where you scored less than three points, and see what factors you're not considering when you're making choices. Do you underestimate the dangers that might lurk in certain situations (choice *B* in question 1, for example)? Do you choose one evil over another, just because

Liz Says:

Some people are bad decision makers in the sense that they make impulsive, stupid, or dangerous decisions. Others just have a hard time making decisions at all. The first one is related to the types of decisions you make. The second is how you make decisions. I am a fairly decisive person, but some of my friends spend tons of time trying to make a very simple decision, like whether they should take the top or bottom gym locker.

one is somewhat less dangerous than the other? In question 2, for example, a crash diet might be somewhat better than smoking, but it's still not the best choice.

18–24 points: Decision Maker Extraordinaire. You're not afraid to take on the big issues, and you have a flair for making smart decisions, even when it might be easier to make another choice. Being a decision maker extraordinaire will serve you well in the years ahead as you face new and perhaps even more complicated life choices.

Do You Have What It Takes to Become a Role Model?

Many experts talk about the importance of girls your age finding role models. But have you thought about whether you could become a role model for someone else? Discover if you have what it takes with this quiz.

1. *You like the feeling of a younger kid looking up to you.*
   ❑ True ❑ False
2. *You can be very patient when teaching a skill that you're really good at to someone who knows very little in that area.*
   ❑ True ❑ False
3. *You can think of at least a couple of people who've been role models for you, so you have some idea what it takes to be one yourself.*
   ❑ True ❑ False

4. *Other people rarely come to you for help since you can seem intimidating.*

❑ True ❑ False

5. *You prefer to skip from one activity to another, without fully learning any of them, because you get bored very easily.*

❑ True ❑ False

6. *When your friends' younger siblings ask if they can join you when you're going skating or bicycling, you hope your friends will turn them down since you won't be able to move as quickly with them tagging along.*

❑ True ❑ False

Liz Says:

I would love to be someone's role model. Hopefully, sometime in the future, someone will look up to me because of the things that I have accomplished. I think that I would be a good role model because I am good at teaching kids skills and can make it fun for both of us. Who knows—maybe I'm already a role model because of the advice column I write online or perhaps because I've written this book. It would certainly give me a good feeling to know that I've helped someone learn or develop in some way, and it wouldn't hurt to know that someone admires what I do.

7. *You find it a pain when people ask you questions about your hobby. If they're so interested, why don't they just try it themselves?*
   ❑ True ❑ False

8. *Your friends often come to you for advice since they know what you have to say is often pretty helpful.*
   ❑ True ❑ False

Scoring

Give yourself one point for answering "True" to questions 1, 2, 3, and 8 and "False" to questions 4, 5, 6, and 7.

Harriet Says:

You can be a role model to someone you know well or someone you never even met. What's important is having qualities that others might aspire to. A person can become a role model without even intending to be one. A former student of mine—from my college teaching days—told me that I inspired her to become a psychologist. It's great to be able to take a little bit of credit for the terrific work she now does with children and teens. Someone can also be a role model for you because she has personal qualities you admire. My mother was incredibly warm, gave terrific advice, and had a great sense of humor. She also loved to write, although she never tried to publish anything. She was certainly a role model for me.

0–2 points: The Unrole Model. Right now, you don't seem to have the characteristics that would make you a very good role model for others. But as you mature, you might become more patient and more interested in helping others. In the meantime, try looking around for people who can serve as role models for you. You never know what might rub off.

3–5 points: Minor League Role Model. You have some qualities that might help you become a role model, and if you're motivated, you can point those other qualities in the role model direction. Maybe you just haven't had many role models yourself, so this is a new area for you. Or perhaps you would rather just wait until you're older to do the role model thing.

6–8 points: Model Role Model. You have just what it takes to become a role model. You're patient, you like the idea of others looking up to you, and you give good advice. All of that is great. Just one warning: Don't get so caught up in being a role model for others that you forget about finding people who can serve as role models for *you*.

Are You on the Path to Success?

There are definitely numerous ways to be successful. What's important is finding the way that makes sense for you—and your future. The questions and answers in this quiz might point you on the path to success that fits in with your needs and interests.

1. *When you're given a school assignment, you:*
   ___ a. figure out how you can do it the easiest and fastest way possible.
   ___ b. try to do it in a way that will teach you something new.

___ c. complete it in the way that matches what you think your teacher wants.

2. *You've heard that taking advanced math and science courses in middle school and high school are important preparation for college and careers. You:*
   ___ a. decide to ignore that advice. Those are two subject areas you intend to stay away from.
   ___ b. will take enough of those courses to get by, but you figure there must be some other more pleasant path to a successful future.
   ___ c. plan to do just that.

3. *Your health ed teacher told your class that sports and fitness activities are important for reducing stress and feeling good physically. You:*
   ___ a. make sure you include working out in your weekly routine.
   ___ b. go to gym class a couple of times a week—isn't that enough?
   ___ c. are so busy with your school work and music lessons that you can't fit one more thing into your schedule. Physical activities will just have to wait until you have more time.

4. *A friend told you that she read an article about how important computer knowledge will continue to be throughout the twenty-first century. You:*
   ___ a. know how to send instant messages to friends online—that's all you really need to know.
   ___ b. plan to take advantage of a computer course your school offers. You agree that the more you know in

this field, the better prepared you'll be for almost any job.

___ c. already know a lot about computer hardware and software, and you look for opportunities to learn more.

5. *You and your family just watched a TV special about the epidemic of sleep deprivation. You:*

___ a. are definitely part of the statistics—you never get enough sleep, even on the weekends.

___ b. try to keep to a regular sleep schedule since you recognize that you don't feel your best when you haven't gotten enough rest.

___ c. sleep in on weekends trying to make up for the groggy state you wander around in during the week.

6. *Many of your friends have hobbies. You:*

___ a. have found a leisure-time activity that doesn't take a lot of time but is something you can continue to enjoy throughout your life.

___ b. get bored too easily to keep at any one thing for more than a couple of weeks.

___ c. prefer to watch TV when you want to relax.

7. *You realize how important friendships are in life. You:*

___ a. make time for friends once in a while, but sometimes socializing seems like a luxury you can't afford because of all the other demands in your life.

___ b. understand the give-and-take of true friendships, and make sure you put real effort into keeping your friendships alive and well.

___ c. spend more time hanging out with friends than doing anything else.

8. *Your parents are constantly talking about how important family ties are. You:*
   ___ a. absolutely agree.
   ___ b. wish they'd stop making you feel so guilty with all that family ties business.
   ___ c. are trying to find the right balance between time with friends and time with your family.

9. *When you think about the way you organize and use your time, you:*
   ___ a. are horrified by how many hours you waste every day, but you don't expect to change how you're living.
   ___ b. generally feel good about the way you divide the hours in the day between schoolwork and leisure time.
   ___ c. realize you should improve your time management skills in a couple of areas, and you intend to do something about it very soon, maybe in a few months.

10. *When you're given money for a birthday present, you:*
   ___ a. immediately and impulsively buy the first thing that catches your eye.
   ___ b. get annoyed since you'd much prefer a real gift.
   ___ c. generally divide up the cash so that some can be saved and some can be used right now for something you'd like to have.

Scoring

1. a: 1; b: 3; c: 2
2. a: 1; b: 2, c: 3

3. a: 3; b: 1; c: 1
4. a: 1; b: 3; c: 3
5. a: 1; b: 3; c: 2
6. a: 3; b: 1; c: 1
7. a: 1; b: 3; c: 2
8. a: 3; b: 1; c: 3
9. a: 1; b: 3; c: 2
10. a: 1; b: 1; c: 3

10–15 points: Lost in Space. Your answers indicate that you are sorely in need of a compass to find your way to a successful future. Yes, you do have plenty of time ahead to challenge your mind and your body, improve your relationships with friends and family members, and develop time and money management skills. But the sooner you put yourself on a self-improvement track, the earlier you'll begin to see results and the more

Liz Says:

In some areas, I'm well prepared to be successful. I use the computer all the time, and I know how important developing advanced math and science skills are. I definitely plan to take those kinds of courses when I get to high school. Fitness is a regular part of my life—I spend about four hours a week dancing and another couple of hours in gym class. Managing money comes pretty easily to me, but managing time is another matter entirely. That's an area I know I need to work on.

deeply ingrained those positive habits will become. Here's one technique that can help you get started: Start a diary (no, not the "That cute boy looked in my direction today" variety) that will allow you to see how you spend your time and money. Just write down all the money you get (allowance, gifts, and earnings) and what you do with it—down to the very last penny. Do the same thing with your time. Jot down what you do with every minute of the day. Keep your diary going for three to five days, and then look at how well you're managing time and money. Often, once you've seen how you spend, save, and waste those valuable commodities, you get a clear picture of where you need to make changes. But if nothing comes through to you, ask an adult for some guidance.

16–21 points: Halfway Home. Your attitudes and actions are pointing you in a good direction, but you might need to do a bit of fine-tuning to prepare yourself better for success. Look at the questions where you lost points, and see what you might be able to do to build a stronger foundation for your future.

22–30 points: Queen of Your Future. Go, girl! You are ready for wherever life might take you. You value strong friendships and family ties, understand how to manage your money and time, and know how to lead a balanced life with time for work and play. Keeping an eye on your future is great, but be sure to leave some of your heart focused on the present, too.

What Careers Are in Your Future?

Do you have any idea what kind of career you'd like to pursue when you finish school? Some girls your age do, but many have absolutely no idea. You have lots of time to explore careers, but your answers to this quiz will give you some food for thought.

1. *Choose three activities you most like to do:*
   ___ a. Solving number problems
   ___ b. Investigating how something works
   ___ c. Visiting a historical site
   ___ d. Using tools
   _✓_ e. Reading books or magazines
   _✓_ f. Listening to a CD or composing a song
   ___ g. Convincing someone to practice good health habits, such as avoiding smoking and drinking
   _✓_ h. Playing on a sports team
   ___ i. Running for a school office or campaigning for a candidate
   ___ j. Creating a poster to get a message across
   ___ k. Learning to converse in a new language

2. *Which three statements best describe you?*
   ___ a. I do better in math and science than I do in language arts and social studies.
   ___ b. I enjoy taking things apart and trying to put them back together.
   _✓_ c. I like figuring out the ending to mystery stories before I've gotten to the conclusion.
   ___ d. I'm the one my friends usually go to when they need advice.
   _✓_ e. I enjoy writing fiction or telling stories I've made up.
   ___ f. I'm often the most talkative member of discussion groups.
   ___ g. I can often convince my friends to follow my ideas.
   _✓_ h. I have trouble sitting still for a long period of time.
   ___ i. I like to do crossword puzzles.

___ j. I enjoy activities like drawing, sculpting, and dancing, as long as I don't have to follow someone else's directions.

___ k. I enjoy parties where I can talk to friends as well as meet new people.

___ l. I like the challenge of figuring out how to put a piece of equipment together.

___ m. I like to do things my way, instead of being told how and when to do them.

3. *Choose the five careers you would be most interested in exploring:*

___ a. Computer programmer

___ b. Lawyer

___ c. Banker

___ d. Public relations (media) specialist

___ e. TV reporter

___ f. Psychologist

___ g. Teacher

___ h. Dentist

___ i. Architect

___ j. Doctor

___ k. Scientist

___ l. Writer

___ m. Salesperson

___ n. Designer or artist

___ o. Engineer

___ p. Newspaper reporter

___ q. Mathematician

___ r. Religious leader

___ s. Photographer

___ t. Researcher

___ u. Librarian

___ v. Social worker

___ w. Manager
___ x. Business owner
___ y. Computer hardware or software designer
___ z. Mechanic

Scoring

1. Circle the careers in the list on the next page that match the letters you've chosen. Have any career titles been repeated? Those are the ones that are at the top of your interest list right now.

Harriet Says:

I've been very fortunate in my work life in that I've always managed to have jobs that have been exciting and challenging. Part of the secret for me has been an openness to new ideas and opportunities. When I was a teen and even younger, I wanted to be a kindergarten teacher. That career aspiration changed during college when I discovered the fascinating field of psychology. That field is so broad that it has allowed me to be an online and magazine advice columnist, a college professor, a manager for a major youth development organization, a book author, a workshop leader, a curriculum developer, a program evaluator, a consultant, and a researcher. Unlike some people who pursue one career and then switch to another one, I usually do several things at the same time. I'm very busy, but I'm never, ever bored.

- a: Mathematician, teacher, banker, economist, stock-broker, computer programmer
- b: Scientist, architect, engineer, psychologist
- c: Teacher, travel agent, travel writer
- d: Architect, carpenter, lab technician, mechanic
- e: Editor, magazine writer, reporter, movie or book reviewer
- f: Musician, singer, dancer
- g: Designer, teacher, doctor
- h: Athlete, coach, fitness trainer
- i: Politician, public relations specialist, salesperson
- j: Designer, artist, public relations specialist
- k: Translator, interpreter, travel agent, travel writer

2. Circle the answers that match the letters you've chosen. Again, look for patterns.

- a: Mathematician, scientist, researcher, computer programmer
- b: Computer software or hardware designer, mechanic, scientist
- c: Reporter, writer, doctor
- d: Psychologist, social worker, psychiatrist, counselor
- e: Writer, librarian, teacher
- f: Teacher, salesperson, TV reporter
- g: Salesperson, religious leader, teacher
- h: Performer, salesperson, producer, photographer
- i: Writer, teacher, researcher
- j: Choreographer, artist, producer
- k: Psychologist, teacher, social worker, salesperson
- l: Designer, carpenter, scientist, dentist
- m: Manager, business owner, producer

3. Look at the five career choices you made. Do any of them match your answers to questions 1 and 2? If they don't, think about why the activities you like to do and the careers you say you're interested in are not the same. Perhaps you're feeling pressured to express an interest in a career because it's a family tradition or because you think it's a way to make lots of money. You're going to spend a lot of time working. You might as well choose something that coincides with activities you enjoy.

★★★ Are You Ready to Change? ★★★

Are you happy with who you are and where you're headed? If so, that's great. But you never know when circumstances might change. If they do, will you be ready to take action? What about if you answered no to the first question? That you're not completely satisfied with the direction your life is taking. Are you ready to change? Answer these questions to find out.

1. *If your family had to move next month, you would:*
   ___ a. be the first to get used to the idea and able to see all the positives of the switch.
   ___ b. be able to cope in time.
   ___ c. have to be dragged screaming and kicking from your present home.

2. *If your teacher was transferred to a new school, you:*
   ___ a. would learn quickly about your new teacher's likes and dislikes.
   ___ b. would take a little while to adjust, but eventually you would feel comfortable again.
   ___ c. would be miserable the rest of the year, even if you couldn't stand the teacher who left.

3. *Your parents decide to try a new recipe for dinner. You:*
   ___ a. think it's a great idea that they're trying something different.
   ___ b. are a little hesitant about trying this new meal, but try to taste it with a positive attitude.
   ___ c. know you're going to hate it even before a single morsel touches your tongue.

4. *For years, your family has gone to the same place during the summer vacation. This year, they've decided to try some place different. You:*
   ___ a. are looking forward to experiencing something new.
   ___ b. take a wait-and-see attitude. Hopefully the new place will be fun.
   ___ c. can't understand why your family needs to go someplace different. There wasn't anything wrong with the place you've always visited.

5. *Your best friend just moved out of the country. You:*
   ___ a. know you'll miss her, but you're sure you'll make another best friend before too long.
   ___ b. hope you'll be able to get closer to one of your other friends. You really like having a best friend.
   ___ c. don't even want to see any of your other friends anymore. Maybe you can convince your family to move out of the country, too.

6. *You just found out that you have an opportunity to attend a school with a special program in an area that you are tremendously interested in. You:*
   ___ a. don't really want to leave your friends behind, but you're excited about this fantastic opportunity.

___ b. are really torn about whether you should enroll in this new school. It's a great opportunity, but it may not be easy getting used to new people, new demands, and new routines.
___ c. realize that most of your friends would jump at the chance to attend this special program, but you hate change. You're definitely not going to change schools.

7. *Your physical education teacher announces that a field hockey program is going to start this spring. You:*
   ___ a. think this might be just the new challenge you've been looking for.
   ___ b. have to find out more about this program before you seriously consider it.
   ___ c. can't imagine why anyone would be interested in signing up.

8. *Your teacher recommends that everyone read a science fiction book. You usually prefer historical fiction. You:*
   ___ a. think this would be a good time to broaden your horizons. You know your reading repertoire is getting a little stale.
   ___ b. are not sure you're going to like science fiction, but you'll give it a try.
   ___ c. can't understand why your teacher is making you read something new. You'd much prefer to just keep reading the books you've always enjoyed.

Scoring

Mostly *A*s: Chameleon. When circumstances require it, you're ready and willing to change. Your outlook allows you to greet change with flexibility and enthusiasm. Instead of seeing the down side of change, you search for its positive aspects. Your attitude must be very much appreciated at home and at school now, and the people who work with you in the future will certainly see this quality as a plus, too.

Mostly *B*s: Cautious Changer. You recognize that life is full of changes, and you greet them with a certain degree of caution. It's not that you expect the worst when change happens—you're just not thrilled about the uncertainties that accompany adjustments to your normal routine. You need time to deal with change, particularly when the transformations are huge. As long as you have the time you need to deal with change, you can thrive in a new environment.

Mostly *C*s: Change Hater. You'd do almost anything to avoid disruption to the usual order of things. You're happiest when life just rolls along smoothly. Unfortunately for you, life is full of surprises. But if you were a little more open, you might see that some of those changes could actually be positive. The next time you're faced with change, try to welcome it as an opportunity—to learn and to grow.

Growing older means getting better when you're prepared to adapt to changing circumstances, when you know how to make smart choices in the face of difficult dilemmas, and when you have the support of family and friends. Now is a great time in your life to start getting ready for the opportunities and careers of tomorrow.